Advance praise for Mike Dooley's

Manifesting Change

The material in this book was originally delivered to live audiences during Mike's second world tour, from 2006 to 2008. Mike later published the same material as an audio program. Here is a very tiny sampling of the many thousands of endorsements and testimonials provided by those who've already experienced *Manifesting Change:*

> "I wanted to write something to express to you how profoundly *Manifesting Change* is impacting my life . . . and yet, for perhaps the first time in my life, I am at a loss for words. Let me simply say, thank you for discovering the Truth about who and what and why we exist."

> "My head is spinning; my heart is full! *This* is what life is all about."

> "Your teachings have brought me so much joy, abundance, and love that I cannot tell you how very thankful I am. Thank you for your wisdom, insight, and knowledge of what we can become if we only believe and ASK for it!!!"

"You have reached the pinnacle! We laughed, we cried, we laughed again . . . WOW! We are lifted up to heights we not only never imagined . . . we never knew you could go that high!"

"This morning, while on my morning walk, I plugged in *Manifesting Change* and I GOT IT! I got it at such a level I burst into tears, threw my hands up in the air and shouted, *WOOOOHOOOOO!*"

"I want to thank you for the amazing *Manifesting Change* course. It was a birthday gift from my wife, which has given me the courage to return to work that I love."

"*Manifesting Change* was the best investment I could ever make. My wife couldn't understand why I wanted a CD set for Christmas instead of the weight bench I asked for earlier. I told her we could gain far more from working the muscle in our heads, along with the spirit, instead of the physical muscles of the body improving our outer appearance . . . She gave in!!!!!!! We listen to it together and have already seen change starting to manifest in our marriage, household, and all areas in our lives!!!"

Manifesting Change

Also by Mike Dooley

Notes from the Universe

More Notes from the Universe

Even More Notes from the Universe

Leveraging the Universe and Engaging the Magic

Choose Them Wisely

Infinite Possibilities

To Amanda

CONTENTS

Preface

What a ride this has been! Had I ever dreamed of becoming a writer, speaker, or teacher, I would have considered such thoughts either fantastical or nightmarish, the latter pertaining especially to public speaking. What began as a quest for truth, however, led me to become all three. I've always craved answers about life and how it works, and the pitch in my yearning to understand these things reached an agonizing crescendo during my first year of college, as I bounced from prayer groups to mediation groups to bible studies. I was overwhelmed with questions pertaining to why we are here, why we die, and what we can do with our lives.

Yet this frenetic searching was laden with a gift—whatever we seek seeks us. And, as these things typically happen, with the "student being ready" and all that jazz, Mom, my greatest fan and closest friend, "coincidentally" sent me a few books over the span of several months with subtle notes attached declaring, "You MUST read this!" I loathe reading, perhaps because I do it so slowly (with a mind that races to the point of being unofficially diagnosed with Adult Attention Deficit Disorder), whereas my mother has had a lifelong appetite for books, consuming more in a week than I would be able to read in a decade. But dutifully following her hints, I read each book one by one, and they turned all of my question marks into excited exclamation points.

The first of these books was *The Silva Mind Control Method*, by José Silva, which, incidentally, is about controlling *your* mind, not other people's minds. It absolutely electrified me as I read through the first chapter. Again and again, I was metaphorically slapping my forehead and thinking to myself, *I knew it! I knew it! I totally knew it!* I knew we were unimaginably powerful. I knew our thoughts were the key to our powers. I knew the world had infinitely more to offer those who could awaken from the prehistoric slumber of believing and behaving as if the things of time, space, and matter were bedrock reality.

A week or so later, before I even got into the second chapter (I told you I read slowly), Mom sent her second book, *Seth Speaks*, by Jane Roberts, and this one changed my life forever. I read it cover to cover, at the breakneck speed of one semester, and I was utterly floored. The book not only helped me connect literally *all* the dots that had mattered most to me about life, dreams, and happiness, but it went even further, objectively and simply covering points and concepts on the nature and totality of our very reality that were beyond my wildest imaginings in those days.

I went on to read all of the *Seth* books that had been published up to that point, finishing them by the time I graduated just three years later, which not only established my own speed-reading record, but put an end to my youthful (and at times painful) quest for enlightenment—a search that was to be followed by the next great obligatory leap required of all who wish to live powerfully, magically, and deliberately: *applying* this wisdom of the ages to *my own life, dreams, and happiness.* Basically, taking theory to the streets and *living* it. And so continued my rather common, conventional, albeit more enlightened life.

My first self-test was surviving a very bumpy start to my career as a PricewaterhouseCoopers (PwC) auditor in Tampa, Florida. Nearly fired for total incompetence, I began a visualization program that would impress any avatar, averting disaster at work while "serendipitously" landing myself in the international tax department, which afforded me the opportunity to travel all over the world. Yet six years into the globetrotting, still wanting much more for myself and by then based in Boston, Massachusetts, I resigned. Within a few months, I had teamed up with my brother, a graphic artist, and my mother, who is *obviously* really cool, and we launched our own company to sell my brother's art (and eventually my writings) screen-printed onto T-shirts. Fast-forward ten years: We have sold over a million T-shirts. Yet with sales beginning a sharp decline, we decided to liquidate what remained and go in our own directions while the "getting was still good." This was both a scary and exciting time in my life that will be chronicled later in this book.

It was at this crossroads, and only as a sideline to my desire to continue on as some kind of an entrepreneur, that it actually occurred to me to incorporate my business know-how with what I had learned from applying my brand of time-tested, street-credited wisdom of the ages to my life. Let's face it: we have to pay our bills *somehow.* So, as a budding teacher and an experienced entrepreneur, I considered moving in a direction that would eventually generate sales rather than solicit donations and "love offerings," the latter of which is often customary when the offerings are more spiritually based. I figured this more businesslike approach would be win-win for my customers and me. But lest you think this was all about me getting rich, I should point out that my offerings are like those of many businesses on the internet in that the vast majority of them continue to be free, including my very popular daily emailings, Notes from the Universe (brief reminders of life's magic and our power).

My life today borders on that of a fairy tale, with world tours, exotic adventures, luxurious travel befitting *Lifestyles of the Rich and Famous*, friends on every continent, a *New York Times* bestseller, my own charitable foundation, health, and lots of love. Indeed, what a ride this has been—and continues to be.

And now it's your turn. What I have, you can have. What I've done—coming from where I came from, scared and starting over—is what you can do. There *is* enough for everyone in the dream of here and now, where manifesting change truly couldn't be easier once you understand the nature of the "game" and you begin, perhaps for the first time ever, to deliberately "play" it. Prepare to be astounded.

To the life of *your* dreams,

November 16, 2010

Introduction

Manifesting Change offers my most in-depth material to date on the *workings* of all things time and space. I'll literally take you behind the curtains of time and space as you know it, revealing how you got here, who you really are, and how to immediately begin creating major life changes. In addition, you'll learn the *objective* metaphysical mechanics that bring about every physical manifestation, including the two most important things you can do to trigger life's magic, place yourself within reach of an all-loving and conspiring Universe (which I'll expound upon in just a moment), and accelerate the arrival of all that your heart desires.

Yes, you read that correctly. In your hands is a book on *metaphysics*. Yikes! Yet what was formerly categorized as "occult" in bookstores is finally, and deservingly, reaching the mainstream—"deservingly" because there's never been anything "woo-woo" attached to the meaning of metaphysics. Per the *New Oxford American Dictionary*, the definition of metaphysics is: *the branch of philosophy that deals with the first principles of things, including abstract concepts such as being, knowing, substance, cause, identity, time, and space.* Essentially, it's about the nature of reality and the study of principles from which all other sciences emerge.

In other words, every religion ever known to humankind is a form of metaphysics. Furthermore, anyone who ever ponders the very meaning of life could be called a metaphysician, at least in their moment of pondering. I hope this puts you at ease if you initially balked at the idea of metaphysics. And for edification, let me explain what I mean when I refer to the "Universe."

In the simplest terms, I am indeed referring to God. But because my idea of God bears little resemblance to the God of Western religions, or Eastern religions as far as I know, I'd prefer not to use a word that comes preloaded with meaning to readers. I believe that God, the Universe, or Divine Intelligence, is all there is. I believe that every *thing* and every *non-thing* is God—that there is nothing that isn't God (animate or inanimate, tangible or ethereal, energy or non-energy, thought or vacuum) in this world, or in realms and dimensions beyond. For something to not be God, where would it come from and what would it be made of? And so I believe that we too are literally *pure God*, you and me. Of course God is infinitely more than what we consciously know ourselves to be, but this doesn't negate that we are pure God, just as a drop from an ocean is pure ocean. We are sparks of divinity come alive in a dream of God's making, and as thinking, choosing, free-willed beings, this dream is also of our making. We are the eyes and ears of Divine Intelligence, in time and space, here and now. So my use of the term Universe can be likened to that of a metaphor for our greater self—the rest of who we really are.

All of this, of course, still raises the question: Why are we here? And the answer is: Because we chose to be. Because it's beautiful. Because love abounds. Because our integrity, our safety, and our *ultimate* joyful reunion with our greater self is assured. Because we'll learn, grow, explore, discover, share, *adventure*—all of it adding to what God is. Yet, *there cannot be adventure without believing in limits,* hence the illusions of time and space that make our stage possible and that create the *fantasies* of here and there, now and then, have and have not.

I do not believe we are here to be tested, judged, and sentenced; we are not trial versions or guinea pigs. We are here to taste the bounty and glory of our own creativity. To swim in a sea of emotions that would otherwise be unknowable. The baton has been passed. And while we can ask for and receive assistance, the entire adventure would be defeated if some greater part of us could make our decisions, clear our paths, and live our lives for us.

We live in a kind world with universal principles that are beholden to the commands we issue *vis-à-vis* our thoughts, intentions, and expectations. Here, our thoughts literally become the things and events of our lives. And with such power, we'd have it no other way than to learn of our abilities and responsibilities for ourselves—from ourselves—without external interference. Knowing beyond a shadow of a doubt that *all* will inevitably return from the dream of life to a place of love and acceptance to be one in mind with Divine Intelligence.

The meaning of life, then, is to *live* it. To *be* here. To follow our hearts. Nothing *has* to happen, and there is no one we're *supposed* to be other than ourselves. There's nothing we're *supposed* to do and no one who needs saving. Yet within such meaning, and as the joyful, fun-loving beings that we obviously are, it is most clearly and evidently our prerogative to deliberately shape the lives we lead with our inborn supernatural powers of matter manipulation. Hence, I offer you *Manifesting Change: It Couldn't Be Easier.*

This book also introduces a Matrix I created, which reveals the entire spectrum of reality from which you can choose to manifest change. By using the Matrix to clarify your desired end results, you'll see how to maximize the likelihood of your successes (and even guarantee them in some cases), and you'll understand the by-products, consequences, and spin-off manifestations you may or may not have anticipated based upon your initial choice. I do believe that because of this Matrix, it's probable that I'll be sharing a few concepts and ideas that you've never heard before, some of which are so innovative that it might even seem as though I'm contradicting commonly accepted truths. Yet by the book's end, I trust you'll understand that such "contradictions" simply represent a greater depth to these ideas than has been shared before.

In my previous book *Infinite Possibilities*, I wrote about our beliefs and likened them to sunglasses because our beliefs filter our experiences 24/7 throughout our lives. And as happens when wearing sunglasses, after a couple of hours of wearing your blue blockers, yellow blockers, or the tint of your choice, you actually forget what the world *really* looks like without your beliefs. However, we never get to take our beliefs off the way we can remove sunglasses, and this means that right now, as you read these very words, you have no idea of how the world *could* look other than how you now see it.

And since, spiritually speaking, we've chosen to be born into very primitive times, completely unaware of our divine heritage and innate ability to influence and shape the material world around us, I'd venture to guess that the tint in your sunglasses, which have been handed down to you by generation after generation of well-meaning guardians or parents, includes beliefs about creating change that might sound something like this: *Life is hard. Opportunity only knocks once. The early bird gets the worm. Manifesting change? Good luck!*

My mission with this book is to help you peer over the sunglasses you inherited so that you can see new possiblities of how life can be. And when you do, you'll find that when it comes to manifesting life changes, you'll finally understand how life *really* works—that it's our thoughts, words, and actions programming life's so-called accidents, coincidences, and serendipities. Moreover, you'll see that you're already a black belt at manifesting change. Not knowing the truth about life's mechanics, you simply spent more time reacting to your creations than you did deliberately shaping new ones.

In the simplest of terms, *your thoughts become the things and events of your life.* They always have and they always will. Therefore, by changing your thoughts, your life will automatically change as well. Of course, using your words and taking action are *equally important*, yet both primarily follow *your thoughts.*

As you might expect, there are a few nuances to this concept of *thoughts become things*, such as other people and their thoughts, the "cursed hows" of dreams and desires coming to pass (talked about at length in *Infinite Possibilities*), and *your other thoughts* (that may contradict what you claim to want)—all of which will receive ample attention in the chapters that follow.

Actually, if I were to sum up all that I'm about to share with you in the pages ahead in just a few sentences, they would sound like this:

You are an ancient spiritual being, who not only chose to be here, but who is literally co-creating the stage

you now find yourself upon. Here, all things are possible
and your thoughts literally become the things
and events of your life.
And this, being a creation amongst your own creations,
is as good as it gets, because whenever you don't like
what's before you, you can change it without hindrance
from the past or so-called "contracts" you no longer
remember! There are no other rules for manifesting
change. There are no hidden agendas for your time in
space. No tests, no destinies, and no judgment. Neither
are there any mysterious, unknown variables working
against you in this Garden of Eden, this paradise we
temporarily get to call home, where manifesting change
could not possibly be any easier than defining what you
want in terms of its end result, and then simply and
physically moving in its general direction.

Like the daily Notes from the Universe that I write, the material in this book is designed to slip past your defenses and into your heart, planting seeds that will blossom into illumination, action, and life changes. It will help you understand *what* you really want, *why* you really want it, and *how* to go about getting it with confidence.

You'll come to understand that your positive thoughts are 10,000 times more powerful than your negative thoughts; that you chose this lifetime to *thrive*. And you'll be absolutely convinced of your power, your worth, and the true ease of commanding forces in the unseen that are freely available to all.

You're not alone. You're being guided. You are unimaginably powerful. You already have all that you need to create all that you want. You can virtually coast from here . . .

A Note from the Universe

Young souls look to secrets, rights, and rituals.

Mature souls look to science, math, and evidence.

And old souls look within.

Look within,
The Universe

PS—Aren't young souls cute?

1

You Are an Effortless Creator

First of all, let's make sure we're on the same page with regard to the truth about the nature of our reality. For me this chapter's title pretty much says everything you need to know: you are an effortless creator. But it would be a mistake if I assumed that what this means to me is the same as what it means to you.

If you go into a bookstore and browse the self-improvement titles on the shelf, you'll find the two-step, or the six-step, or the twelve-step programs to "success," but in virtually every case, the authors assume that the readers share their worldview, which is rarely true. So first, I'm going to do my best to ensure that you do indeed understand the truth about the nature of our reality, your place in it, your power, how you got here, and what you can do with your time in space.

I've just completed a U.S. book tour for *Infinite Possibilities* that included more than seventy radio station interviews. Interestingly, although perhaps predictably, the one question that surfaced again and again was this: "Mike, what do you think the number one thing is that keeps people from living their dreams?"

My reply was always the same: "Not understanding the nature of our reality, who we are, and the actual mechanics that bring about change."

People have a lot of questions when it comes to God, spirituality, religion, and purpose, and it gets all the more confusing when you throw in misunderstandings about karma and the New Age concepts of abundance and the law of attraction. And immediately, with such confusion, they begin to unwittingly give away their power.

What good is it to resonate with the law of attraction and to believe in an all-conspiring Universe, yet simultaneously believe that God is watching and judging you, or think that karma might undermine your dreams for achieving perfect health, or that your desire for abundance is somehow sinful or recklessly selfish?

Happily, yet ironically, the truth is objective and easy to grasp. The nature of our reality is deducible, knowable, and very simply this: we are creators, alive in a loving Universe—spiritual beings who live in a world of illusions that we have not only created but still exercise control over. The focus of our chosen attention is what shifts the circumstances of our lives around. That's it. Case closed. There's no hell, judgment, or New Age ideologies that mitigate this power. There is no such thing as a destiny to follow, dues to pay, or penance to offer.

Until very recently, people have refrained from asking the hard questions about who we really are, how we got here, and what we can do with our lives out of fear of stepping on God's toes, or because we've just been too busy surviving. Yet by finally asking such questions, which is now starting to happen in every corner of the globe, we find, lo and behold, that there *are* answers—answers that make sense, that resonate with us, and that, above all, are easy. It's just that most of the answers are not quite what we might have expected them to be, to the point that they even appear blasphemous to those heavily rooted in old-school thinking.

I want to devote this entire chapter to exploring your power and grounding you in truth, removing any question marks you have in the tapestry of your understanding through which your power could ebb away. I want you to have no doubt about your role in the creation of your reality. To this end, so that you're not just taking my word for the perspectives I offer, I'm going to share with you the simple tool of deductive reasoning and how it helped me move toward "enlightenment." It can help you—in your own way, at your own pace—connect dots, answer questions, and get your groove on.

The Search for Bridey Murphy

When I was fourteen years old, two things happened that really rocked my world—two things that I can share with you, that is. The first is that I discovered a book in my school's library called *The Search for Bridey Murphy*, by Morey Bernstein.

Connecting Dots

To backtrack a little, prior to this literary discovery, I had already begun my quest to understand life's biggest mysteries. I didn't find answers at home, at school, at church, or in the community, so I started looking along the so-called fringes of society. For me, books on ESP, telepathy, hypnosis, Bigfoot, and UFOs hinted at greater realities that, if understood, might give time and space more meaning. Not that I could read many books on these subjects, given how slowly I read, but each one I did manage to read excited me beyond measure.

By the time I turned fourteen, I was already beginning to draw conclusions about the hallowed jungles of time and space. What I was doing, unbeknownst to me, was simply using deductive reasoning to arrive at a form of spontaneous illumination. Of course, I didn't use any of these words since I didn't know this was what I was doing; I would just think about something logically and then intuitive answers would come to me. Unfortunately, I had no confirmation that my answers ever remotely approached the "truth"—until I discovered *The Search for Bridey Murphy*.

I remember saying to my mother back then, "Time just can't be *real*." I hypothesized and reasoned that if you were to put a human lifetime (of say, one hundred years) on a timeline stretching to infinity in both directions, in an instant you'd see how a human life becomes absolutely immaterial in the grand scheme of things—virtually nonexistent and inconsequential. Of course, subjectively, we can most certainly attest to the reality and significance of our lives. But to make this juxtaposition even more obvious, realize that if you took the largest number that could possibly be generated by the most powerful supercomputer today (imagine atom-sized number nines stretched from here to Pluto and back), then multiplied that number by seventy-two zillion and put the result on that same timeline stretching to infinity in both directions, in an instant that number would virtually *disappear* too, swallowed up by eternal time to become virtually nonexistent and immaterial. Something's going on. For time to be real, these numbers just don't add up. And by the same analysis, incidentally, neither can space be real.

I shared other insights with Mom as well. I told her, for instance, that clairvoyance and telepathy must have some validity. Just one example of this is that there are numerous documentaries on television of ESP studies in which people in one closed room can pick, with some degree of accuracy, flash cards that someone else was looking at in an adjoining room. I pestered my mother with other conclusions too, sparked by numerous stories in the media and books that revealed the power of our thoughts and subconscious mind. These included stories about subjects going under hypnosis and spontaneously demonstrating other bizarre abilities, such as speaking a foreign language, and programs on telekinesis, astral projection, and spoon bending. Now, I'm not giving skeptics very much here, but only an extreme doubting Thomas could patently denounce any and all forms of telepathy, ESP, or mind power. Clearly, there's something huge going on that the mainstream is unable to completely understand or explain.

The Case for Reincarnation

Another deduction, I reasoned (and I have no intention of ruffling any religious feathers), sprang from my religion's claim that we live only one life. Even as a fourteen-year-old kid, I knew that just didn't add up. And I ask you to go within and ask yourself, does this make any sense? Does that claim resonate with you? Both science and religion state that eternity exists in one facet or another (however illusory). We can even sense that there's something eternal in our nature and spirit. And given all of this, why would we live only one lifetime? If your best friend was born in the Sudan during a drought and famine but you were born in Beverly Hills, you'd have to think, "Oh man, bummer! I am so sorry. Geez, one life *out of eternity*, and that's all you got? Too bad."

What if, however, as spiritual beings, we live as many lives as we want to? Wouldn't that make sense if we have eternity to play in? Wouldn't it make sense that you'd want to try out some male energy and some female energy? You'd want to come here with an analytical left-brain disposition one time, and then perhaps you'd like to try out being right-brained and artistic. You might want to be born into primitive times, technologically and/or spiritually speaking, and then you might want to be born into advanced times. After all, *you've got forever*! Do you realize that you could live seventy-eight trillion lifetimes, and when you were done, you'd still have eternity leftover? These were some of the ways my fourteen-year-old brain worked and these conclusions of mine made sense to me, but again, until reading *The Search for Bridey Murphy*, I had no outside confirmation that I was anything other than a wild daydreamer.

Corroboration

The Search for Bridey Murphy is a true story about a hypnotherapist who took a patient back in time to get to the root of her migraine headaches. In their first session, he regressed her a couple of years, and although they didn't find the cause of her migraine, he was astounded to discover that she had complete and total recall of the day he took her back to. She could describe her clothing, what she ate for breakfast, who else she spent time with, and the conversations she had. With no success discovering the source of the migraine, however, they scheduled another session.

At the next session, he regressed her further and with the same result: total recall but no solution to the migraines. Session after session after session, he took her further back in time until she was recalling herself crawling around on the carpet as a baby, describing it and the room in detail. The hypnotherapist then had the brilliance to wonder if he could take her back even more, and sure enough, she began describing conditions in the womb: fluctuating light, temperatures, sounds, even voices. He then had the wherewithal to take her back further. Now *that's* thinking outside the box! And sure enough, she continued to have total recall.

She began describing a buoyant, light-permeated atmosphere filled with friends. She described her existence as one of conversation and travel. The hypnotherapist asked her, "Friends? Places to go? How do you communicate with your friends?" And she replied, "Thought. Everybody knows what everyone's thinking." She was talking about *clairvoyance*!

He then asked her, "Places to go? How do you get there?" And she said, "You think about them and you're there." Ah-ha! *Mind over matter! Our thoughts give us wings!* Reading this, for me, was like winning at some kind of philosophical slot machine. *Cha-ching, cha-ching,* with one *Aha!* moment after another.

He took her even further back and she began speaking with an Irish brogue, describing another life in Ireland. Yes! *Reincarnation!* He took her back between lives and to another life before that. Page after page, chapter after chapter—I was in ecstasy. Of course, while receiving enormous recognition, this book also received enormous criticism when it came out. But I ask you: Does this make sense to you? Does it resonate with you? Chances are, it does. BIG time and for a reason: *this is what it feels like to discover the truth!*

Incidentally, many years later, I finally stumbled across *Many Lives, Many Masters*, by Brian L. Weiss, MD, which not only offers virtually identical parallels to what's shared in *Bridey*, but also shares the discovery that there were indeed references to reincarnation in the Old *and* New Testaments that were deliberately stricken in the sixth century!

Ask and It Shall Be Answered

Then came the second thing that rocked my world when I was fourteen. I decided to share *The Search for Bridey Murphy* and my new insights with the grown-ups I knew. And the worst possible thing imaginable happened: *they didn't care.* "Oh, Mike, that's interesting." "Oh wow, really? Cool . . ." "Don't you have homework to do?" No one cared, and I remember feeling totally scandalized. I couldn't understand then (or now) how and why *anyone*—even the greatest minds among us!— couldn't be as excited and enthralled as I was to discover personal accounts (most of which highly correlate to one another) that hint at the deeper fabric of the life we know. How could one not wonder about experiences that support the concept of our essence existing independently of not only our physical bodies but also the physical world?

To this day, I think to myself how unnecessary and unfortunate it is that people don't bother to consider the deeper implications of life. "Unnecessary" because it's so easy to go within, connect a few dots, deduce new insights, and resonate with a previously undiscovered truth, which, once uncovered, gives your present life even more meaning. These discoveries can instill confidence and give peace. They can allow us to be more certain of our power while hinting at how to use it. And invariably they can enable us to fall even more in love with the gift of our very "being."

The truth is, you *are* eternal, powerful, and supernatural—and there's evidence of this everywhere in your life. Yet if you don't ask questions about life's greater truths, discovering and leveraging them will likely involve both hits *and* misses.

A Note from the Universe

Nobody on this side of the curtains of time and space would ever dream of telling anybody on your side that they've got their beliefs crossed, that they're kidding themselves when it comes to relationships, that they're not seeing "the obvious," or that they're not asking the tough questions. Uh-uh, nobody over here's going to do that. Could you imagine? We'd be labeled critical, judgmental, and non-supportive!

Besides, we don't need to. The system in place works just fine. Everyone discovers truth in one of two ways: either through introspection, going within and connecting just a few dots; or through the manifestation of chaos.

Win-win!
The Universe

The greater point is that just as you can go within for enlightenment on clairvoyance or reincarnation, so can you go within for enlightenment on your own unique life situations! If you don't—if you're not your own instigator and don't take the initiative to reveal and then use your magnificence, whether prodded by pain or curiosity—chaos likely awaits.

Focus your attention on the areas of your life that you're not yet pleased with, go within, and connect a few dots. Illumination will eventually follow.

I'm stunned by how few people ask the bigger questions for themselves about who they really are and what they can really do with their lives. Even professional people who've mastered their trade—doctors, lawyers, bankers, butchers, bakers, or candlestick makers—often still march in lockstep with their parents and forefathers, adopting the same ideologies and spiritual beliefs as if there were no other option. If they would just take the time to apply their brilliance by going within and asking some questions about the areas of their lives that aren't "working," they could literally astound themselves.

I once wrote a Note from the Universe that speaks to this, which at the time I thought was a bit abrasive, but I sent it out anyway and no one complained. So, I'm going to share it with you:

A Note from the Universe

You might never guess it, but sometimes, even here, we get frustrated. The classic case happens at homecoming parties when we hear the guest of honor lament, "Gosh, but I had no idea! I never would have guessed! I didn't know I was so powerful! I didn't know I had such an effect on others! I didn't know I was so responsible for my thoughts, words, and deeds! I just didn't know!"

But it's even worse for them when we reply, "Yes . . . but you could have."

Of course, we follow that up with something much lighter like, "Hey, you look fab in wings!"

Tallyho, The Universe

I remind myself of this Note constantly. It's a good kick in the butt because I'm just like you: I'm an adventurer. I've got stuff to learn and things to master on this journey, and there are times when I spin my wheels and perhaps lament about something, thinking, "Dang it! How come this keeps happening?" or "Why am I getting so angry?" or "How come I'm not making the kind of progress I envisioned?"

And I have to remind myself that it does no good trying to do the same thing again and again, expecting a different result. Finally, I ask myself, "What am I not seeing that's obviously there? How else could I view this situation?" And this is all anyone needs to do to begin a new adventure into truth.

Deductive Reasoning: Drilling Down to the Truth

Let me say a little more about deductive reasoning. *Time Magazine* once commented that the hallmark of Albert Einstein's genius was that he could figure out complex problems and equations simply by thinking about them. When I read that, I was a bit indignant because I thought, "I do that!" And then I realized, "Wait a minute, *everybody* does that," or at least, everybody *could* do that. Except that we've been taught from the time we could walk that in order to expand our minds, we must get more schooling and read more books. But that advice is based on the presumption that knowledge exists *outside* of you. None of us were taught to go *within* ourselves when we want to learn something or solve a problem, yet that's where the greatest wisdom lies.

Roughly speaking, deductive reasoning works like this: let's say you know with certainty the truth about *A* and the truth about *B*. By going within and contemplating these truths, it turns out you can then deduce, with certainty, the truth about *C*. And this becomes really exciting when you then know the truth about *D* and *E*, because you can now deduce the truth about *F*. It gets even more exciting because now that you know the truth about *C* and *F*, you can continue *ad infinitum*. It turns out that there is *nothing* you can't deduce by first going within. And the reason I'm mentioning this is because going within should be your starting point when answering questions that may be vexing you. Whatever it is you want to know, go within. And best of all, you generally have to connect only a few dots, not all of them, to arrive at your answer.

When I'm conducting workshops and I get to this material on deductive reasoning and spontaneous illumination, I share a child's connect-the-dot puzzle of a mystery beach animal. Before connecting the dots, *no one* can guess what the creature is, but then I show the puzzle again, this time with *fewer than half* of its dots connected, and there's an instant leap of recognition. Spontaneous illumination occurs, and suddenly there's no one in the audience who doesn't know with certainty what the mystery beach animal is: a rhinoceros!

Some of my audience members have later told me, "Mike! You cheated! No one finds a rhinoceros at the beach," but that led to an unintended lesson of this little exercise. Most of the time— if not *all* of the time—the answers we're having trouble finding that concern the "tricky spots" of our life are *not* what we thought they would be. This is why we had trouble finding them. Invariably, the question to ask when stumped is: "What am I not thinking of that I could be thinking of?" Or put another way, "What am I not considering that's otherwise obvious?"

The *intended* lesson, of course, is that we only had to connect *fewer than half* of the dots for spontaneous illumination to take place. And this is what I want to convey concerning those areas of your life where you're stuck in the mud, or not making progress: *ground yourself in the truth, recall your ancient heritage, consider the unexpected, go within, and connect just a few dots.* You don't have to unravel your entire life, figure out who you were in the fifteenth century, or use subliminal, subconscious programming. Just connect the dots that you can to gain, rather miraculously, an entirely new perspective with which to understand whatever was frustrating you.

A NOTE FROM THE UNIVERSE

Would it be enough to know (and you can know this through deductive reasoning) that long ago, when the two of us carefully mapped out your pending adventure into the jungles of time and space; the hills and valleys you would traverse; the setbacks and advances you would encounter; the good, the bad, and the ugly, and all of the lives you would touch; when our planning was done and the big picture was revealed . . .

You burst into tears of joy, overwhelmed with its perfection and who you'd become.

Yeah, like a baby.
The Universe

PS—I'll never forget it because I cried too.

Getting to the BIG Picture

Okay, let's do some deductive reasoning together. I think that by now you're probably on the same page as me; you grasp that time is an illusion, meaning that it's not bedrock reality. Of course, both time and space have a reality *within their confines*, but in the bigger scheme of things, they are not bedrock reality. Einstein expressed this in his theory of relativity: time and space are experienced differently from one person and one situation to the next; or in other words, they're illusory and subjective. Are you with me?

The Source

From this premise, let's connect one more dot. If time and space are not bedrock reality, doesn't this mean that both spring from a deeper reality that existed before them—pre-time and pre-space? Yes, it *must* mean that. Now that we agree that a reality precedes time and space, let me ask you, what would you find there?

Now *this* is a question in which it seems there could exist 72 trillion dots that make up the answer, so it's understandable that you might look at all of those dots and be absolutely overwhelmed (and then look at your watch and realize you have places to go, things to do, and no time to spend connecting dots). This is what happens in life. Most people are so overwhelmed when looking at the biggest picture of reality that they don't deduce what is otherwise *obvious*, or what is otherwise readily deducible.

I'm going to connect one dot right now that you'll totally agree with, even though just a moment ago you probably drew a complete blank when I asked what you'd find in the reality that preceded time and space.

Awareness Is God Is Thought

You would find awareness—Divine awareness, if you will: "God," the Universe, or Infinite Intelligence. You'd have to, unless you think that there's no intelligence to our presence here at all. And if there's no intelligence here, this *must* mean (and some have concluded as much) that we are the random product of space dust that collided billions of years ago that somehow evolved into consciousness, eventually clawing its way out of the ocean before ultimately learning how to walk upright, invent language, write books, and read. Good thing we've already nixed this as an option when we agreed that time and space cannot be bedrock reality. They're illusions and hardly a suitable place for space dust to ignite into consciousness.

All of this must mean there's a reality that preceded time and space, and we can now deduce that there *must have been* awareness. (Please indulge me as I make time-based references, such as "precede" and "must have been," even while speaking of non-time settings! Words fail in such instances, yet we do the best we can.) And what is awareness by definition? *Thought!*

Bringing It Home: The Face of God

Hold on because now we're about to blast off: if there was once nothing but thought where there now exists solar systems, planets, continents, oceans, and mountains, what must it all be made of? *It must all be made of thought (or at least a derivation or form of thought)!*

MIKE DOOLEY

And there's one more parallel dot we can connect here that will put you in your power and seat you on your throne. If, where there was once only Divine Awareness, Divine Intelligence, or God, there now exists you and me (among all others), *who must we be?* We *must be* the eyes and the ears of God: pure God ourselves! Suddenly, the answer is patently obvious, and we arrived at this by simply connecting *a few dots* with our deductive-reasoning minds.

To help you see the simplicity here, consider this: just as you can't enter a kitchen with raw potatoes and carrots and return an hour later with an apple pie, neither can you begin an "equation" with 100 percent pure God and end up with something that's not 100 percent pure God. We *are* God, come alive in the illusions of time and space. You are divine. You are holy. You are 100 percent pure God. There's not an atom of your illusionary body or your own thoughts and awareness that can be anything less than pure divinity.

You are *of* the creator, *by* the creator, and clearly an *effortless* creator *now*. You can't even stop creating because you can't stop thinking, and thought is what everything is made of! You have the exact same properties as Divine Mind, Divine Intelligence, Divine Awareness, or God. In no uncertain terms, each of us is, in a sense, a Mini-Me of the Universe! And *this* is where your power comes from.

A Note from the Universe

Do you think, as the Universe,
I would have created a world and inhabited it
to learn that there are some things
I can't have, do, or be?

16

Do you think I'd make mountains that couldn't be moved?

Do you think I'd feel love that couldn't be returned?

Do you think I'd have dreams that couldn't come true?

Or do you think I would have made pretty darn sure I could kick butt there too, no matter who I came as, no matter what schooling I'd received, no matter what age I found myself to be, and no matter what others thought of me?

Yeah, baby.
The Universe

PS—Talk about "Easy Buttons."

Lights, Camera, *Passion*

I can imagine that your mind might be rumbling right now, and you might be thinking, "Wait a minute, Mike. I don't remember creating the sun, the moon, and the stars. I hardly recall what I had for lunch yesterday. How could I be the eyes and the ears of the divine?" *As if not remembering something could take away what is easily deducible and readily obvious with just a little bit of thought!* Further, with a little bit of deductive reasoning, it's easy to understand why you've deliberately forgotten your role in the creation of your corner of time and space.

Consider, for instance, watching a movie in the middle of the afternoon. Do you want the lights on or off? You want them off, don't you? Why? So you can see the film better, but

17

not just with your eyes. You want to see it with your heart. *You want to feel it!* You want to be gripped with passion by the scenes. You want to strive. You want to struggle. You want to overcome. You want to fall in love with Cameron Diaz or whoever is on the screen. With the lights turned off, you can temporarily and comfortably forget who you are because you know it's only for ninety minutes or so, and by the time it's over, *in the blink of an eye*, you'll be back to so-called reality, back to living your life. Yet for having experienced the movie, even while forgetting yourself, you'll nevertheless be entertained, educated, and enriched. Actually, you're going to be slightly changed by the experience, and I'd venture to say always for the better, even (or especially!) if the movie wasn't what you expected.

It's the same with life. You don't have to remember how you got here. You don't have to remember charting your course, setting the stage, or choosing your parents to know that you did (I'll help you get to *that* one by connecting a few more dots in just a moment). And similarly, you *can* grasp that not remembering something doesn't necessarily negate it. After all, do you remember beating your heart over 2,000 times since you began reading this book? Do you have to know the thrust-to-weight ratios that make aviation possible in order to sit on a plane and enjoy the ride? Do you have to know who turned on a light in a darkened room to make use of that light? No. And neither is it important that you remember crafting the moments that led you to today in order to know that you had a role in crafting them. By realizing you are a divine creator, even without remembering how it is you've created thus far, you can still find your mojo, chart a new course, and take command of your life and manifestations.

The Evidence

Of course, there will still be those who'd prefer some tangible proof. No problem! Our lives are proof of everything I've said—proof of our spiritual nature and of our incredible power (a power wrought by choosing the thoughts we think). We've all witnessed time and time and time again how our thoughts have become the things and events of our lives. Plus, we just deduced that if there now exist solar systems, planets, continents, oceans, and mountains where there was once nothing but thought, then all of it must be made of thought, right? *Well, look who's thinking now!*

> *The hardest thing to explain is the glaringly evident which everybody had decided not to see.*
> ~AYN RAND

Think of how your life has unfolded up until now. I would bet that for 95 percent of all the major events and circumstances of your life, whether it was where you went to school or when you stopped going to school, where you decided to work or where you decided not to work, who you decided to marry or who you decided not to marry, you can recall thoughts, imaginings, or visualizations of their outcomes, all of which preceded those experiences. Your life is proof enough, and for the 5 percent of things that you cannot yet explain by the end of chapter 7, "Understanding Adversity," I think you'll understand why.

Thoughts become things fully explains how we have *indeed* been given dominion over all things. They're *our* thoughts; *we* get to choose them. And as we choose, so move heaven and earth. It's the be-all and end-all process for creating change in your life. It's the be-all and end-all for living the life of your dreams. *Thoughts becoming things* is inviolate. *Your* thoughts— *your* focus—*your* power!

Explaining the Law of Attraction

Thoughts becoming things is *why* there is a law of attraction. *Thoughts becoming things* is the primal mover, the first principle, the Holy Grail! And best of all, phrased this way, we immediately see where we fit into the equation of reality creation as effortless creators for the thoughts we choose.

Think about gold coins magically appearing in your hands. Why don't the coins materialize if *thoughts become things*? That is the literal interpretation of *thoughts becoming thing*s, but we live in a reality continuum shared by six billion other people, and it has a track record, physical laws, and a lot of momentum that we've all come to abide by and trust. Manifesting gold coins out of thin air would violate the beliefs and expectations of those we share this continuum with, not to mention shatter many physical laws that, for now, we're quite happy to give precedence to.

So instead of manifesting these things out of the ether, *something even more miraculous happens*. Once you have a clear picture of something—anything—in your mind, there is an instantaneous *attraction* working within physical laws and cooperating with your beliefs and expectations of whatever you're thinking about (as well as with those who would be affected by your manifestations), hence the law of attraction. Our thoughts have an energy and life force all their own, which literally rearranges the players and circumstances of our lives and predisposes us to the so-called accidents, coincidences, and serendipities that *will* yield our brand new manifestations.

In this way, our thoughts *literally* (but not instantaneously) become the things and events of our lives as circumstances morph them into place, taking millions of other variables into account. There are no mitigating factors to this power of our focus—not karma, not angels, not ancient spiritual contracts. These concepts have their place, speaking to certain truths and attempting to explain certain phenomena in time and space, but none of them trumps our ability to choose our thoughts. And nothing gets in the way of our thoughts subsequently becoming the things and events of our lives, other than our own thoughts in contradiction, including those beliefs, public and private, that define what is possible.

You are an effortless creator because you effortlessly think, and your life is a living testimonial.

A NOTE FROM THE UNIVERSE

If there was just one thing I could tell you about living the life of your dreams, knowing that it would be enough if you understood it, I would ask you to realize that you already are.

In the presence of greatness,
The Universe

Getting your groove on begins with understanding *who* you really are, and this will make all the difference.

And Then There Was You

Before we wrap up this chapter and get to the core material, I want to lead you through one more sequence of deductive reasoning conclusions that will yield new illuminations, revealing your heritage, your power, and how and why you got here.

If you now understand that you are of divinity; that you are pure source energy, pure Universe; that you emerged from the totality of Divine Intelligence *which preceded* time and space; then you can know that you, or some portion of yourself, *also preceded* time and space, and knowing this, you can connect one more *stunning* dot.

If you preceded time and space (and you did), that means there's only one plausible explanation for your presence here and now in the these illusions: *You chose to be here.* There's no other explanation. You came first. You were not an afterthought. You were not an experiment. You were not pushed off of a cloud. You did not draw the short straw. The only way Divine Mind gets or goes anywhere is if Divine Mind *wants* to. You can know this with certainty, intuitively and intellectually.

Better still, there's more we can deduce about this decision. If it was made prior to your self-imposed amnesia setting in (not recalling all that led you to choose time and space), you can be certain that this decision was made from the zenith of your magnificent awareness and divine brilliance. And having been made from this glorious vantage point, you can know it had to have been one heck of a beautiful decision, made for outrageously compelling reasons. It's not important that those reasons may escape you now, though they could be deduced eventually. You can still rather effortlessly deduce, as we've just done, that it had to be the case that you were acting from a "place" beyond genius, and from *there*, you chose *here and now*.

This means that you picked the stage you'd play your life upon, all to further the adventure. Not that anything is set in stone or predetermined, but this stage was chosen for the potential it held to challenge *you*, thrill *you*, and teach *you* what *you most wished to learn*. You knew what "buttons would be pressed" by this choice to be you, and you wanted them pressed—the good, the bad, and the tricky.

Moreover, you can know with absolute certainty, based on the dots we just connected, that you, exactly as you are, with every freckle and blemish, are *who you most wanted to be*! Divine mind does not take chances; it doesn't need to. It's a ridiculous notion. You didn't stand in line saying, "Okay, I'm up for time and space! What have you got left?" You designed, with meticulous attention to detail and perfection, the "person" now reading these words—the "who" you have become.

If you can grasp that you are of divinity, by divinity, and divine yourself, then there is no other plausible explanation for your presence here other than your choice to be here exactly as you are. And this, more than anything else, can remind you that all is well, that you are exactly where you should be, and that you knew *exactly* what you were doing.

With this kind of thinking, coupled with your conscious ability to deliberately summon illumination via the tool of deductive reasoning, there needn't be a time in the remainder of your life when you're feeling so trapped, perplexed, or vexed that you can't go within, connect a few dots, and begin peering over the sunglasses you've been wearing heretofore to see how else you might view your life and circumstances.

A Note from the Universe

*It's as if you're pounding on the massive doors of the kingdom of
your wildest dreams. At first lightly, even respectfully, then, losing
patience, louder and louder. You pray. You plead. You beg. You ask.
You cry. You wail. And just on the other side of the door, your
faithful, adoring subjects silently writhe, some quietly crying,
all intensely feeling your frustration and loneliness.*

*Yet they remember all too well how, on the day you left,
you made them swear not to ever open the door,
so that you might discover for yourself . . .*

. . . that it was left unlocked.

*I hate when that happens,
The Universe*

Why are you reading this book? What doors have you
been pounding on? I'm happy to tell you that, no matter what
they are, they're unlocked, and by connecting just a few dots
and expecting the unexpected, you'll find the illumination
you're seeking; you'll be able to glide on through into a brand
new, exciting world. Rest assured, the truth is within you, as
are the answers to the questions you're now asking.

You Can Do This!

Let me share a little exercise that I do all the time. Simply jot
down as many examples as you can of different dreams or
thoughts of yours that have already become the things and

events of your life. Create this list by skipping lines so that every other line on the paper is blank. (You can start by using the sample list below.)

Once you've made your list, use the alternating blank lines to jot down current dreams of yours that *will* one day come true.

This simple act of associating prior successes with successes you wish to experience will empower and remind you that you've been there before. It will remind you that turning your thoughts into things isn't something new—that there are no tricks to learn. You're already a master when it comes to working your manifestation muscles as an effortless creator. No one has to learn how to make their *thoughts become things*; they just need to awaken to the fact that they already do in order to purposefully and deliberately harness their natural-born, matter-manipulating skills.

My thoughts that have become things:

A slight variation of this exercise is to write down fears or challenges from the past that you've overcome. Then, intermingled within that list, write down some of your present-day fears or challenges. Again, this simple act of associating prior successes with current hurdles will immediately show you that you've been there before. This is not new territory. You can do it again.

If you want to experiment with a third variation of this exercise, you could write down a long list of people who have achieved as you wish to achieve, and then add your own name somewhere in that list. For my list: Dr. Wayne Dyer, Dr. Deepak Chopra, Fabio . . . Mike Dooley—*yeah!*

These exercises are so simple, as are others I will share with you, but don't underestimate their power. This is all about creating mental images of the successes you seek. Anything you can do to *remind* yourself of your power, *align* your thoughts with the life of your dreams, *live* the life that you'd like to live, and *be* the person you'd like to be *is powerful*. Take a moment now and start making your lists.

2

The Miraculous
Mechanics of Manifestation

Just because the mechanics of manifestation are indeed of a miraculous nature doesn't mean they need to be mysterious, and they most certainly are not. In this chapter we're going to move into the heart of the book by looking at an overview of what actually happens that brings about all change. This is where we will first peer behind the curtains of time and space to appreciate that virtually all of the invisible mechanics that bring about change are mechanics we program from our side of the curtains. In other words, we'll see that the Universe (or "life's magic"), taking its cue from our conscious thoughts, words, and actions, literally grabs the baton and runs, performing innumerable, incalculable, and mind-numbing "miracles" that eventually turn our thoughts into things.

The Greatest Secret

When I was creating this material, I thought: what better place to begin a talk on the miraculous mechanics of manifestation than with the very first manifestation ever, *the jungles of time and space*? Don't you wonder how they all came about? Don't they boggle your mind? Don't you wonder at the intelligence and brilliance that had to have measured out all the details—the *spectacular* beauty, the *impossible* perfection, and the *infinite* vastness?

Did you know that modern-day scientists estimate that there are more than one hundred *billion* stars in the Milky Way Galaxy *alone*! And further, they conservatively estimate there are at least 100 billion more *galaxies*! That's ten sextillion stars or more, not even counting planets. Yet, on this floating space emerald that we call home, scientists also estimate that there are at least one hundred million different species inhabiting air, land, and sea—of which humans are just one. Every crack, crevice, nook, and cranny on this planet is teeming with life!

Did you know that there are microorganisms that thrive in hot lava pits? Did you know that there are whales off the eastern coast of Canada that communicate *by song* to whales 2,000 miles away in the Caribbean Sea? Did you know that there is a bird (the Arctic Tern) that takes off every year from Siberia at the onset of winter to fly 8,000 miles away to warmer weather in Australia, doing much of its flying *while it sleeps*? And in our own backyards, parks, and gardens there are caterpillars that fall asleep only to wake up as butterflies! *Isn't it amazing?* Don't you wonder how it all came about? Have you considered what kind of mind could have fathomed the details?

I used to ask myself these questions when I'd take a break from writing, kicking pinecones around my backyard for my dogs while pondering, to the point that my brain would sometimes ache. And then one day, as if struck by lightning, I got the answer. It gave me total peace. I'll never have to ask those questions again. And in the days that followed, I excitedly wrote that insight down as a Note:

A Note from the Universe

Ain't it grand? Doesn't it boggle your mind?
The harmony, the splendor, the beauty, the intricacies,
the synchronicities, and the staggering perfection?
Do you ever wonder how it all came about?

Do you think I studied quarks, atoms, and molecules?
That I drew schematics for the sun, moon, and stars;
the otter, Gila monster, and penguin? Do you think I
painted every zebra, flower, and butterfly?

Or do you think . . . I simply imagined the end result?

And that's all you ever have to do!

Yeeeeee-ha!
The Universe

PS—I hated school!

The line "Or, do you think . . . I simply imagined the end result?" holds the greatest secret of the miraculous mechanics of manifestation: *The entire process happens in exactly the reverse order shown to us by our physical senses!*

The Universe didn't think small and then think bigger and bigger and bigger. The Universe didn't sit down and say, "Oh my gosh, *science*! Almost forgot science. We're going to need biology, chemistry, physics, quantum physics—oh—*and math*. We're going to need *a lot of math* for reality!" No, the universe wasn't assembled on a timeline! Though that's how we typically assess any creation—using our physical senses alone, thinking in terms of beginnings, middles, and ends. *Completely forgetting that time is an illusion.* Instead, the Universe simply began with the end result: the spectacular beauty, the impossible perfection, and the infinite vastness. And in that *instant*, all of the mathematics, all of the sciences, everything necessary to support life as we now know it in time and space, fell into place. *In an instant!*

The greatest secret of the miraculous mechanics of manifestation is that the entire process happens in exactly the reverse order shown to us by our physical senses. In other words, an imagined ending point *forces the means* that will bring about the manifestation. Or even more simply stated, thought *forces* the ensuing circumstance that will yield the brand new manifestation.

The starting point of all creation, and certainly with any change we wish to manifest, is *with the desired end result in mind.*

The Three Steps for All Manifestations

You could say that there are three steps to all manifestations, whether we're talking about the Universe's manifestations or yours and mine. The first two steps are our responsibility, while the Universe takes care of step three. Our parts are the easy parts!

Step One: Define what you want *in terms of the end result.*

Step Two: It's incumbent upon us to *physically move* in the general direction of our dreams. By physically moving, you ramp up your belief in the inevitable manifestation of your dream. Moreover, you put yourself in a place of receivership.

There cannot be happy accidents, lovely seren-dipities, or so-called coincidences if we're just sitting on our couches with a vision board, waiting for Oprah to call!

"Must" is an ugly word, but *if* you want to see change in your life you *must* move in the general direction of that change. That's easy! You don't have to figure, calculate, and carry the weight of the world on your shoulders. Just do your best to physically move in the general direction of your dreams, which I'll clarify in the pages ahead. Once you do steps one and two, the Universe does step three.

Step Three: The Universe creates a brand new manifesta-tion in a brand new *now*.

This is a bit jarring because we don't expect the process to culminate in a brand new *now*. Usually, we think the journey begins *now* and finishes later. However there are two ways that *now* expresses itself or can be sensed: the *ethereal now* that contains the thoughts you think, and the *physical now* that is made up of the world around you. The starting point of all physical change is in thought, which is the only "place" the *power of now* exists.

The Power of Now

If you look at the illusions—all things defined by time, space, or matter—surrounding you at this moment, are they not the result of yesterday's journeys and end results? Similarly, if you want to change your life in physical terms, the starting point must be in thought, with *a new end result* in mind, followed by a new journey. This is not an intuitive approach if you've historically relied on your physical senses, which in large part explains why making deliberate change up to this point has been a very daunting task for most people.

Most people think the *power of now* lies in the *physical* moment, made up of the circumstances or world presently surrounding them, so they start their journeys here and now *physically*. They believe that it's only natural that to get from physical point *A*, where they are starting from, to physical point *B*, where they dream of going, they need to manipulate all things time, space, and matter—the illusions—to do so. They also think they need to introduce themselves to Mary, who knows Betty, who's doing the interviews for the job they're after; they think they need to put themselves in the right place at the right time. However, this approach is nothing more than messing with the *cursed hows* (worrying about and trying to force *how* their dreams and desires will come to pass) that I spoke about at great length in *Infinite Possibilities*.

The reason people do this is because of their initial misunderstanding of where their power lies, thinking that it's in the now of the illusions, justifying their messing with the *hows*, so that *one day in the future* their dream will come true. But if you see your dream coming true *one day in the future*, that's very often where it stays. Like a carrot on the end of a stick, as you move through time, your dream is always just a little out of reach. Instead, see the new and desired *end result* in your mind's eye *as if you are living it now*. Not in some near or distant future.

Your vision then begins attracting itself to you as life's magic, programmed by your chosen end results (step one of the process), puts the right people in the right place at the right time on your path. You just need to be physically "out there" in the world (step two), showing up where you can be reached. The Universe, that greater part of you (or more accurately, the metaphysical laws of the Universe), will always do the hard part of then figuring out (forcing) the *hows*, which is the virtually incalculable part (step three).

All we have to do is define whatever it is we want or the changes we wish to experience *in terms of the end result*. Define them *as if you were already there* (which is what visualizing is all about, as you'll see later in this book), and then simply begin moving in the general direction of your dreams, knocking on doors and turning over stones.

Before My Very Eyes

Allow me to deviate a moment to share with you an instance in my life when I witnessed these mechanics of manifestation unfold before my very eyes.

One Night in Riyadh

It was more than twenty years ago, when I was living in Riyadh, Saudi Arabia. One evening I had spent some time with friends riding horses in the desert. Around 9 PM, I said my goodbyes, moseyed on over to my car, and began what would normally be a thirty-minute drive home on one of the city's many superhighways, which were virtually deserted at this hour. Twenty minutes into that journey, traveling at about fifty miles an hour and thinking I was the only car on the road, there was a sudden flash before me. Another car had run the traffic light. I didn't even have time to hit the brakes before broadsiding it.

The "Impossible" Perfection

Sitting on the curb, dazed, battered, and confused, while waiting for what would be a fleet of paramedics, police, and ambulance vehicles, I was suddenly struck again! But this time, it was metaphorically, with a realization of the mind-bending *manifesting perfection* of what had just happened.

By that time in my life, I was long past believing in "random" occurrences like accidents, coincidences, and serendipities. Yet this belief meant that the choreography necessary to get me in exactly the right place at exactly the right time for this "intended" collision to happen was mind-boggling.

Now, because this stuff excites me so much, I did some math and want to share it with you. Traveling at fifty miles an hour, you are literally *flying* at seventy-five feet *per second*. Imagine that. Plus, taking into account that I hit a moving target traveling at about the same speed perpendicular to my path, this would mean that had I arrived at the intersection *one tenth of a second* earlier or later, the two cars would have *completely* missed one another! By one tenth of a second!

By deduction and inference, this means that if *anything* had happened differently on my journey to affect my arrival by *one tenth of a second*, the "accident" would not have happened. If I had gotten off my horse just a little bit more slowly, or if I had walked just a bit faster to my car, or if I had fumbled for the keys in my pocket, or if a fly had flown into my car and distracted me *by one tenth of a second.* Or if I had, say, listened to more buoyant, happy music and consequently driven just a tiny bit faster, the two cars would have completely missed one another.

And continuing by inference, if anything that *entire day* had unfolded differently—if I had woken up with a sore throat; or if my alarm clock had gone off late or I had forgotten to set it, I would have likely stayed later at work to make up for my tardy arrival—and there would have been no collision. If anything in that entire week had gone differently, such as being called off to Jeddah or Cairo or Ta'if on a business trip that didn't bring me back in time to ride horses that night, then the two cars *would have completely missed one another.* And if anything in that entire month or year had changed. . . . Are you beginning to see it too? The perfection? The impossible, *absolutely impossible,* perfection of choreographing such a sequence of events!

The Explanation

This choreography *is* impossible *if you interpret reality with your physical senses alone;* impossible *if* you think circumstances are what give rise to more circumstances, instead of understanding that it's our thoughts that force the circumstances of our lives; and impossible *if* you think time-space events are crafted along a linear timeline. But the perfection that evening in Saudi Arabia over twenty years ago was *effortlessly possible* if you just peek behind the curtains of time and space, where you would see that the entire event was designed without these illusory constraints, beginning with the end and working backwards!

Only by beginning with the end could you then figure out exactly where I would have to be one tenth of a second before impact. Only by beginning with the end and working backwards could you then calculate where I would have to be four and a half minutes before impact and what my speed was, my mood, the music I was listening to, and so on, *ad infinitum*. Only by beginning with the end and *working backwards* could you even place me at the riding stables that night.

Like in the Movies

This "beginning with the end" concept isn't actually new for you if you've ever seen a Hollywood movie. Are they crafted and manufactured on a linear timeline? Never! Oftentimes the end of the movie is filmed before the beginning, yet always, the key pivot points of a movie are filmed first. Once these are captured, moviemakers can cut and splice the film, and determine the segues between one event and another, so that when moviegoers *watch the film on a linear timeline* from the comfort of their theater seats, the entire production makes sense, with a logical beginning, middle, and end.

Similarly, for all time-space manifestations, the details are calculated, orchestrated, and packaged in the unseen, beyond the timeline in which we "later" experience them. We only perceive them later with our physical senses, often scratching our heads at the accidents, coincidences, and serendipities that seemingly occurred as if by magic. Granted, for some readers, I've now stepped in to some "woo-woo" territory, but what's the alternative? That we live in a world where random things happen to random people in an otherwise mind-bogglingly perfect, stunningly breathtaking, orderly theater?

We experience the physical world on a linear timeline, but this is not where it's constructed. It's all constructed in realms we can't access, triggered by our thoughts of new end results. These end results, combined with steps taken in their general direction, literally make all of the segues *inevitable*—all of the details, players, circumstances, and "luck" necessary to pull off a manifestation that mirrors what you were originally thinking about. And here's the kicker: in Riyadh that night, during the entire twenty minutes leading up to the point of impact, I thought *I* was alone and in control!

Now, did I just imply that there are some aspects of our lives that we have no control over? And did I earlier imply that our physical lives are packaged for us? Yes! Enter . . . the *cursed hows*! *Cursed* only when we try to control them. *Pure magic* when we surrender to these logistics of creation.

Programming the Hows

Our brains are far too small (no offense) to be able to deal with all of the invisible intricacies that bring a manifestation to pass. However, we have complete and absolute control over *the end results we choose*. In other words, we have total control of our thoughts and what we choose to focus on, and this is what triggers the mechanics of manifestation, turning unseen wheels and making gyrations, calculations, and so forth, to yield a brand new manifestation. It's our end result that commissions the forces of the Universe to figure out the *hows*, and as long as we have end results and are *taking action in their general direction*, the entire Universe will unfailingly be thrown into motion at our behest.

It's just like when you rent or buy a movie. You have total control over the title. You can change your mind at a moment's notice. You can decide on the genre, rating, or actors you want to see, but you have no control over the dialogue and plot twists, which is very often why people watch movies in the first place! Similarly, in time and space, you can pick the genre, the types of players, the general nature of the scenes, all of which you have total control over, yet how they arrive and how it all gets packaged and sewn together is beyond our ability to grasp, other than to simply show up and experience it. The point being, even though we have little to no control over the *hows*, we have the supreme power to choose our end results that will set those *hows* into motion for us.

We have to put the desired image of what we'd like to experience "out there" in thought and *hold on to it*, even though at first the physical world seems unaffected, so that there can later be those changes. And finally grasping this will instill within you the patience and confidence necessary for you to begin enjoying the journey (and the wait), giving universal principles the opportunity to do their part, however long they may take.

Why a Car Crash?

The questions bouncing around in your head right now might be, "Geez, why was there a traffic accident? Was this your end result? Was this something you were thinking about or dwelling upon?"

The cause

Whenever the seemingly "unthought-of" unexpectedly lands in your path, it is always a steppingstone to another place that you *have been* thinking about. This is worth repeating:

whenever the unthought-of is experienced or manifested, it is always a steppingstone (or a *how*) to another place that you have been thinking about. In the traffic accident, there were several long-range end results that I *was* thinking about that could perhaps be best achieved effortlessly, flawlessly, and miraculously through this incident, which I'll share in just a moment. To be clear, however, I'm not implying that anything could happen on our journeys. We're not victims of fate or chance or luck. Anything and everything that does happen on our path would fit in and be predicated upon *all* of our other thoughts.

Still, I know that I'm using a traffic accident to illustrate the miraculous mechanics of manifestation instead of sharing with you some of my more exciting manifestation stories, but there's a good reason for this.

If you've read *Infinite Possibilities* or if you've seen my *Thoughts Become Things* DVD, you've heard me talk about how I once created a scrapbook, like a vision board, whereupon I pasted pictures of foreign, exotic destinations that I wanted to visit one day. And then I share how two years later, this young, unassuming accountant (me!) from St. Petersburg, Florida, suddenly found himself at the Regent Hotel in Kowloon, Hong Kong, looking through two-story, plate-glass windows at the very view of Hong Kong Island that I had put in my scrapbook just two years earlier. I could have shared that story with you instead of the car crash.

Or I could have shared with you my stories about creating abundance, or stories about finding and creating fulfilling work, international travel, or love and relationships, but *none* of those stories would have revealed the *exacting* nature of the Universe's hand in our affairs like the traffic accident does!

With a traffic accident, you can instantly grasp the difference *one tenth of a second* makes between seeming bliss and seeming catastrophe. And then you realize that there's no tenth of any second in your life when the Universe isn't there controlling and manipulating the players and circumstances you're facing based upon *your* thoughts, *your* end results, and the actions *you're* taking. And this can give you the confidence to empower you when you finally begin to deliberately exercise your own manifesting muscles, knowing that you're never alone.

The effect

I achieved at least two end results that I'm aware of through this traffic accident. First of all, from the age of eighteen to twenty-five, the latter being when this accident happened, I was on the ridiculous treadmill of going out almost every single night, looking for parties and the "cool" people. I was always afraid I would miss something, so I would stay out late and I'd come home exhausted.

At 6 AM, my alarm clock would go off and I'd be regretting that I went out the night before. I'd ask, "Why do I do this? It's so pointless." But then the evening would eventually roll around, and I'd be running out of the door again, not wanting to miss anything. Well, after that traffic accident, which was a near-death experience for me, I was off that wheel of late-night partying and early-morning regrets. I can't explain why it changed me, but after that event, I had no problem telling my friends, "No. I'm going to pass tonight." Even on the weekends, I'd happily stay home. I was "cured." I achieved what I wanted—my goal, my end result: not going out and not perpetually feeling like I was missing something or someone cool if I stayed at home and got a good night's sleep.

Ironically, the car that ran the traffic light was carrying Prince Abdulaziz bin Abdulaziz bin Abdulaziz al-Saud, the great-great grandson of the founding king of Saudi Arabia! Talk about catching up with the in-crowd, huh? Very funny, Universe.

The other end result I achieved through this accident? Well, I wasn't kidding when I said that while sitting on the curb after the accident, I was metaphorically struck again with a realization of the stunning perfection I had just experienced. My entire life (to that point), I'd been joyfully obsessed with understanding the nature of our reality, forever wondering at its mechanics and pining to know more—to unravel its mysteries and discover its secrets. Well, *vis-à-vis* this "accident" and the resulting stream of thoughts that poured through my mind while sitting dazed and confused on the curb, my wish was granted. I truly got to peek behind the curtains of time and space.

In that moment, it suddenly dawned on me that *if there is no such thing as an accident*, then the logistical mechanics, the choreography, and the production required to hit this car exactly as I did, even though I couldn't physically see it coming, *boggles the mind*!

A Question for You

Now, you either believe in chance or you don't. And if you don't, which I suspect is the case, then consider *any* prior manifestation from your own life and ask the question: "If this occurrence didn't happen by chance, then exactly what were the mechanics, the logistics that made its manifestation possible?"

Invariably, you too will see that the manifestation was made possible through a series of events that could *only* have been calculated and assembled in the "unseen." And once you *see* this for the first time yourself, you'll realize that, when it comes to manifesting deliberate change in your life, you must always have the end in mind as your starting point, followed by physically showing up, so that you're in a place to receive life's unending miracles.

The greatest secret of the miraculous mechanics of manifestation is that the end in mind forces the logistical and physical means, including the people and circumstances, that will bring about its manifestation: exactly the opposite of how our physical senses interpret events and manifestations. *Thought forces circumstance.* To help this become even easier for you to comprehend, and to move away from the esoteric, let's look at a few other practical examples.

How Do They Do That?

The Athlete

Consider Tiger Woods for a moment, *as a golfer*. He does the "impossible." I remember watching him on television when he was playing a tournament in Kauai, Hawaii. He and the other pros had just driven their golf balls off the coastline, over a stretch of ocean, and onto a tiny island that held the putting green, cup, and flag. On this particular day in Kauai, there were gale-force winds so strong that their roar in the cameraman's microphone was almost the only thing audible to viewers at home, except the flapping of everyone's trousers on the green, which sounded like flags in the wind.

Tiger was about forty feet away from the pin—a long putt even for Mr. Superhuman—but he lined it up, as he always does, and let that putt go. Even over the roar of the wind, you could hear the few people on the green gasp, because Mr. Amazing was going to be about fifteen feet off the mark! It was a *terrible* putt—until, of course, the ball rolled onto its first nearly invisible rise and began self-correcting toward the hole. Then it suddenly began over-correcting. You could hear another gasp, as it again appeared to be a *really terrible* putt, about twelve feet off the mark in the other direction—until the ball rolled onto its second nearly invisible rise and began self-correcting, at which point almost everyone knew that this was going to be another classic Tiger Woods putt. The ball neared to three feet away from the pin and started slowing down . . . two feet and slowing further . . . one foot away from the cup and slowing down even more. With the wind gusting, that ball stopped two, maybe three, centimeters away from the cup. I was in complete awe, and all the people on the green were cheering. And then, suddenly, the wind blew the ball all the way in!

That's *impossible* golf! *Nobody can do that.* The human body, mere flesh and bone, cannot calculate with its tiny little brain all that needs to be calculated to pull off that kind of putt under those kinds of gusty, *unpredictable* conditions, yet Tiger pulls off that kind of putt tournament after tournament, month after month, year after year. Why? Because Tiger has an end result: "*I am a world-class, below-par professional. I am a champion. I am number one!*" And that end result starts the principles of the Universe working backwards from the vision, putting him in the right place at the right time. He thinks he chooses his tournaments, but I'd beg to differ; the Universe is riding shotgun. Its principles are micromanaging—steering him into tournaments; choosing the ideal clubs, coaches, and caddies; and handling all of the other *countless* variables.

The Universe and its principles are there every second of every day for Tiger, just as they are in every second of every day in your life, forcing the circumstances; the epiphanies; the new people; the good, the bad, and the ugly so that you'll experience manifestations in time and space that mirror precisely what you've been thinking about (and moving toward) most.

The Universe works backwards. The Universe starts with the ball in the cup. The Universe knows where the wind is going to be, even though it's gusty and unpredictable to us on a linear timeline. The Universe works backwards, considering every detail—even the direction the grass is growing on the green as it leans toward the sun at the precise moment of the day when the ball is hit. The Universe takes into account how far the swing should go, how heavy the club is, how much power is needed, and what angle the face of the club should have when the ball is struck. The Universe does the virtually impossible—*IF* we can hold on to our end results and move toward them in spite of it often seeming like nothing is happening.

Tiger moves toward his end results by simply playing golf and doing what other professionals do, and then the Universe fills his sails with inspiration and bright ideas on how to play better and achieve his end results. The Universe works backwards, meeting you far more than halfway!

The Salesperson

How is it that any sales office always has one or two team leaders in closing sales? No matter the office, company, or country these people are in, every month of every year it's usually the same people leading the pack. They're not better looking or more popular than anybody else, yet they're always in the right place at the right time.

The explanation for being successful in any facet of life has nothing to do with good looks and popularity. Those who succeed in sales or anything else have an end result that makes it so. They have an end result that they're the masters at closing the deal, or perhaps they see even further than that. Perhaps they see themselves living a life of splendor in wealth and abundance, and *instantly*, with that as the end result, the Universe knows how to get them there.

The Universe effectively says, *"I know how to do this! You're in sales! "* And then that person will always pick up the phone at exactly the right time, whether it's to make a cold call or to receive one from Switzerland, and that call will make his year. He can answer the phone with a Big Mac in his mouth while listening to Bob Marley, and the right person will still appear at the right time, the proper words will be chosen, and the deal will be done. Confidence will be instilled, beliefs fortified, and repeats get even easier. The Universe orchestrates the details flawlessly, far beyond our comprehension, as long as we can hold on to the end result and move with it. For a salesperson, moving in the general direction of his dreams is simply a matter of going to work and doing what his peers do, yet once he understands these mechanics (or even if he doesn't but he happens to "work them"), the hard stuff is taken care of automatically! Yet if he knows what he's doing, he can then relax, enjoy the journey, and dance life's dance, making cold calls, networking, and the like—doing his part *so that the Universe can then do its part.*

The Author

How is it that J. K. Rowling or any bestselling novelist is able to spin one enthralling yarn after another? It's because Rowling and others like her have an end result that says, "I am a world-class storyteller; I am a bestselling novelist." And as they go through the motions to move in that general direction, simply writing on their computers, contacting agents, maybe hanging out at book fairs, *everything will be given to them.*

I like this example because it illustrates that it's not just players and circumstances that are rearranged on our path when we have a new end result. It's not just the agents or the publishers or the readers that are taken care of with precision for J. K. Rowling; she is literally *infused* with the levels of inspiration and creativity required to pull off such a tall order. Creativity and bright ideas—these are *given to us* when they're necessary to achieve the end we've been imagining and moving with. Where do you think *your* good ideas come from? You have never had a single bright idea that you didn't summon as necessary to achieve an end result that you were already thinking about.

When you understand this, you can summon the next great invention, the next great story, the next great business idea, the next great teaching model, the next great parenting technique, or whatever your line of "work" calls for. If you have an end result that could not otherwise be brought about without you having an epiphany of some sort, you will then be provided this bright idea *gratis* on a silver platter as you go about your affairs and move—physically move—toward your end result.

Incidentally, it's not just creativity, inspiration, and motivation that we're handed when we have a new end result. The person who believes and declares (demonstrating their focus and end results) that life is hard and people are mean, or that all they have to do is see food to gain weight—well, the Universe can play those games too. What you're thinking and speaking will not only draw about players and circumstances, it will even bring about feelings that help hasten the manifestation of whatever you're dwelling on. If your end results and related thoughts, *intentional or not*, don't serve you, those feelings will be of helplessness or even depression. We summon these mind-sets by our chosen perspectives, and our perspectives are nothing more than the end results or the thoughts we choose.

Fortunately, the really good news is that you can turn your ship around on a dime. This is the classic story of the prodigal child from the Bible. In the instant that truth is recognized, you are welcomed back into the fold, and life begins working *for* you instead of against you. Simply begin with saying things, thinking things, and dwelling on a new end result that will serve you, such as: "My life is easy! I love my life! I have so much free time!" First create the reality within your mind.

The Tycoon

How is it that the rich keep getting richer? First and foremost, contrary to everything you've ever been told, there is no connection between intelligence and accumulating abundance—none, *zippo*. Just look at many of the people who have wealth! The rich get richer because they either have the courage or the audacity or the brilliance or maybe even the naïveté to hold on to an end result that says, "This could happen to me! I see myself surrounded by abundance!" They then take the all-important step of simply moving in that direction by maybe researching investments, talking to the kind of people who might be able to give them ideas, networking. Whatever it is that they do, as long as they *consistently* move in the direction of their abundance dreams (including following job leads that could play a role), and as long as they hold that vision in their mind, it *must* come to pass. They cannot stop it; that's how powerful these universal principles are.

Cracking the Money Nut, Losing Weight, and Being Photogenic

Now, of course, this works in the opposite way as well, because there is often that person who comes to me and says, "I get 'thoughts becoming things.' I love my life. I love my wife. I've always been a positive person, but, Mike, I just can't crack that money nut!" Oh, no. You *cannot* ever expect to crack the money nut by saying that you can't crack the money nut! Your words are a declaration of your thoughts. Your words— your focus and attention—reveal what your true end results are. And if you're walking around telling me or anybody else that everything is cool but you can't crack the money nut, then you will never crack the money nut!

What about the person who tells you that they want to lose weight but just can't? *They're right!* They're absolutely right because the same universal principles that put the stars in the sky will conspire to show them that they cannot lose weight, and they will be put in the wrong place at the wrong time, predisposing them to the wrong foods, undermining their confidence, making them feel powerless, and keeping them in a reality in which they *cannot* lose weight.

Once again, there's an upside to this. You can immediately begin turning your ship around by simply starting to say new things—things that serve you—such as "I am surrounded by wealth and abundance!" or "Everything I touch turns to gold!" Whatever area of your life you'd like to change, start speaking as if you've *already* achieved it: "The pounds are just disappearing! It's never been this easy before!"

And don't forget this one: "I am so photogenic! I can't take a bad picture!" Say it; it works. This example is from personal experience. I used to be one of those people who'd say, "Get that camera out of here. Don't take my picture. I hate my pictures!" Until one day, as crazy as it sounds (and sometimes this stuff does sound crazy), I experimented with saying the opposite, and wouldn't you know it, my pictures are now fantastic!

Remember to say these things even when they're not true at first. In fact, *say these things especially when they're not true!* This is why you're saying them! Don't worry that it seems weird. Of course it does, especially compared to the way you've approached sparking life changes before—the old fashioned way of focusing on what you don't like and what doesn't work. But how successful were you then?

Anybody worth $20 million can say everything they touch turns to gold. It takes a spiritual maestro, however, an absolute enlightened genius, to be able to make these sorts of statements *and then move with them*, if in no other way than pretending—in spite of evidence to the contrary that may surround them (their $60,000 of credit card debt or the sagging stomach). It takes an enlightened genius to hold on to such a vision, move with it as your end result, and not lose faith in spite of what's happening in your world. All of which becomes infinitely easier to do when you *understand* the mechanics of manifestation—because then you understand that you don't have to figure out the *cursed hows*, you grasp that you've been working miracles since you could crawl, and you realize that there's a system that will do the hard parts of manifesting for you.

The Trick Lies in Understanding

Again, understanding is what we're after. Understanding is the elixir of life. Understanding how life works puts you in a place of power. With unanswered questions and apathy, you give away your power; it ebbs away from you. You become impotent and incapable of making the changes you want simply because you've got questions about whether or not you're worthy to have what you want—if you've done enough; if you just need to be luckier; whether or not you chose this lifetime to experience poverty (I've actually heard that one), or whatever misfortune you think you're experiencing.

No one is here to experience a poor life. No one is here to be sick. No one is here to be lonely. Wherever your life started is not necessarily where it's supposed to stay, unless you say so. You came here to thrive, and while you also chose challenges, it was on the sole condition that each and every one of them would be surmountable. And the best way to surmount them, and fast, is by understanding the truth.

The truth I'm sharing with you now is that *the end in mind* is the starting point of change, and it's an end that you must hold on to and physically move with, especially in spite of any contrasting circumstances around you.

You Can Do This!

Your "homework" is to start saying things that serve you as *if* they were true. In other words, you're going to start saying stuff that serves you especially when it's *not* true. You're going to say things that your contemporaries would deem crazy, so don't share them; just tell them to yourself, the mirror, or while sitting silent in your car. Say them, feel them, believe them. And as this material unfolds, you'll see that I'm also going to ask you to start predicating your behavior upon that vision playfully—as in make-believe. It really couldn't be easier.

Please use the following table as an icebreaker and then continue making similar lists on your own. Think through what you'd like to change in your life and how you'd like to change it, thereby giving yourself ready material for declaring what will be true in your life, as if it was already true.

Statements asserting that you are already the person you've always dreamed you'd be, getting the love you've longed to have, doing the things you've wanted to do, having the friends you've envisioned having, and visiting the places you've always dreamed of visiting:

MY IDEAL LIFE *NOW* LOOKS LIKE THIS:

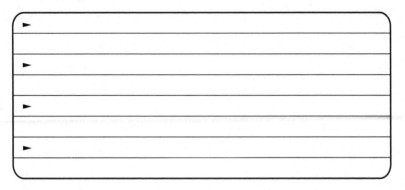

3

Do Try This at Home

We've gone from theory to real life examples in my over-view of the mechanics of manifestation, but because grasping all of this is so fundamentally important when it comes to making deliberate life changes, let me share what I believe to be a near-perfect analogy that should absolutely clinch your understandings.

I think you probably know about MapQuest.com, one of the many websites that give driving directions to any address you provide, and if you don't live in the United States, I know that there's an equivalent to MapQuest in virtually every country on the planet. The first thing you tell the web-site is the physical address of your starting point, where your journey will begin. The second thing you tell it is . . . *your end result*! And in the *instant* you give it your end result, it calculates every possible road you could travel on. It takes into account yields, merging lanes, speed limits, stoplights, *everything*, and in a heartbeat returns to you the shortest, quickest, most harmonious way for you to get there. In other words, it calculates the *hows* for you in a split second, and this is exactly what the Universe does when you give it a new end result. It instantly knows the entire sequence of events neces-sary to get you from where you are today to the manifestation of this end result. And this sequence will begin to play itself out *once you start moving*.

Like MapQuest, there are now digital satellite navigation systems you can buy, or that come built in to high-end cars, that read the GPS satellite signals wherever you are. With these systems, you don't even have to give your starting point. The system already knows—much like the Universe knows—where you are at any given time. The whole process begins when you specify your desired destination, or end result, from which these systems will literally speak through your car's stereo speakers to guide you through the route, telling you when to turn left or right until you arrive!

Manifesting Your Own Miracles

Let's recap how we can bring about our own miracles as we parallel our understanding of the miraculous mechanics of manifestation with how a digital satellite navigation system works.

1. Possess a clear end result.

First and foremost, when it comes to manifesting your own life changes, a clear end result is critical. As miraculous as a direction finder is, it can't help you until you first tell it where you want to go. Furthermore, you must *accurately* tell it *exactly* where you want to go, being as clear as possible. If you make a one-digit mistake in the zip code, you could end up in the wrong state. If you type in apartment A instead of B, you might end up knocking on Bruno's door in the middle of the night instead of Babette's! Clarity in life, especially when it comes to manifesting change, is priceless, and I'll share more on this in subsequent chapters, including some insights for those who feel they aren't even sure what they want.

Having to purposely set your end results also speaks to the importance of honoring *your preferences* and having dreams— whether they're material (and nothing's wrong with that) or not, and there's no reason you can't have both. You must have a reason to get out of bed every morning and a direction to move in, even though in our old-school society, we've been instilled with an inborn fear of being selfish, simply because we have wants and desires. In actuality, it's our wants and desires that make possible and give meaning to our holy pilgrimage through time and space—enabling Bill Gates, Bono, or Hillary Clinton, for example, to shine their lights the brightest onto the darkened paths of others as they pursue what they most want to pursue. And no one can know what moves in your heart or stirs your being better than you. *The first step in making your dreams come true is having them.*

A NOTE FROM THE UNIVERSE

Roger. You have been heard.

You're always heard, every single thought,
and at this very moment, every single atom in the cosmos
is being reprogrammed, every single angel has been summoned,
and big wheels are a-starting to turn!

We just hope you weren't kidding.

Ungawa,
The Universe

There's no room for kidding. You're always being watched. Universal principles are always at play. And when it comes to choosing your end results and deliberately shaping your life, it's up to you to decide exactly what your priorities and preferences are.

2. Move in the general direction of your dreams.

You must (the ugly word again, but you *must*) physically move in the general direction of your dreams to ever see them come true. I can't tell you how many people have come to me after a talk and said something to the effect of, "Mike, I've watched *The Secret* eighty-two times; when is my life going to start changing?" And the sad news is if that's all you're doing, your life's not going to change. It's incumbent upon us to move, to take action, to be within reach of life's magic and in a place of receivership.

It's not enough to get in your high-end car with its fancy GPS system and give it an end result. Not even an "I *love* you, baby; I *believe* in you, baby; I have *faith* in you" is going to help. Nor will proceeding to rub your gratitude rock, giving thanks and oozing gratitude all over the place. If this is all you do, your car won't move one inch! Your navigation system won't be worth its weight in scrap metal. At least not until you *put your car in gear and physically move*! Not putting your car in gear tells the entire system, "Not yet! I'm not ready! I'm still making up my mind! I need to line up my ducks." And whether or not that's what you meant to say (or if, through misunderstanding, your choice is to take no action, or to wait for a "sign" to first be rich, or to have a soul mate on board), then you're giving away your power.

You don't even have to start driving in the correct direction because, as long as you at least start moving, the system can reach out and offer assistance like, "Make a legal U-turn!" And in life, once you at least start moving, you can then be infused with inspiration, sent a new best friend, or given whatever is necessary to help get you back on the ideal path.

Action is essential: first, because anticipation is aroused, which ramps up the belief in your inevitable success; and second, because, as I keep saying, it puts you out there in the world, where you can then experience life's so-called happy accidents and coincidences. Neither of which can transpire when your life is in "park."

A NOTE FROM THE UNIVERSE

I'm so excited! Everything's just about ready!

I've arranged for all the right players to appear at all the right times—big shots, little shots, and some absolute angels. You aren't even going to believe who you'll soon be schmoozing with, or where. I've lined up the necessary phone calls, emails, and chance encounters so that you'll be disposed to waves of loving, inspired thoughts precisely when you most need them. I've calculated, literally to the billionth degree, the pivotal coincidences, happy accidents, and clutch plays that will blast you to heights previously unimagined. I even took care of happily ever after!

So . . . how are things coming on your end?

Ain't life grand?
The Universe

PS—Right. You do have an "end." It's the simple end. Choose your destination and physically move in its general direction.

Only by putting your car in gear does your navigation system know that you're truly ready for the journey, and only by taking action does the Universe, your greater self, truly see that you are indeed ready for change.

3. Remember that the miracles of progress are almost always invisible.

Look at it like this: You just met a new friend at some internet dating site or a business function, and he invited you to his home, which is a two-hour drive from your home in a town or city you have never visited before. On the day you're to visit, you tell your navigation system the end result *and* you put your car in gear. At what point in your journey would you know that every single bit of advice given to you by your navigation system was flawless, miraculous? Right! Only upon arrival or in the very final seconds of the journey, even though with every left or right turn you took during those two hours, *nothing looked familiar and you had to continue on faith.*

It's not as if the more your journey progresses and the more accurate the directions, the more familiar the territory becomes as you approach your end result. Even one minute before your arrival, if you were using your physical senses to interpret your progress, you might conclude that "it isn't working," and be at risk of quitting and going back home!

Every single day, you're getting closer to your dreams, and this needs to be your root assumption. *Just because you can't see the progress you're making doesn't mean you aren't making any.*

Once you've got an end result and you begin moving with it, gigantic wheels begin turning for you behind the curtains of time and space. *It always works.* Don't draw false conclusions by saying to yourself, "Oh, it's not happening for me. It works for everybody else. I don't know what I'm doing wrong. I must have invisible, limiting beliefs." These kinds of declarations (which are also thoughts and end results) will draw experiences into your life that sabotage the progress you were, in fact, already making.

4. Don't override the system.

This is just one more chance for me to advise that you not mess with the *cursed hows*. This system always works. Trust it. Just as when your navigational aid tells you to go north, it does little good trying to outsmart the system. Similarly, don't try to over-calculate or offset what's going on in your life by tweaking people, places, and circumstances. It's pointless to physically observe that "Jessica went south months ago, and she found happiness, so why can't I?" Simply hold on to your desired end result and then get busy dancing life's dance. Don't insist on any one "door" or "stone" being your salvation; by insisting that they be the key, or how your dream will come true, you actually limit universal principles and life's magic.

A Case Study: How I Did It

My End Results and Baby Steps

I experienced these mechanics of manifestation in my life about ten years ago when Mom, Andy (my brother), and I decided to liquidate what remained of our T-shirt and gift business. I had enough money to coast for a couple of years, so I decided to start knocking on doors and turning over stones, with my intended end results being: (1) wealth and abundance, (2) friends and laughter, (3) international travel, and (4) creative, fulfilling work (not necessarily in that order). That's all that I was going to insist upon (and we'll talk more about why end results are best when they're general in nature).

Next came step two in the manifestation process: moving in the general direction of my dreams. When I began knocking on doors and turning over stones, one of the first doors I knocked on was creative writing. I still had the domain name of tut.com, and I was still sending out weekly emails for free, so I thought I'd explore this further to see where it led.

The weekly emails soon turned into daily emails, which evolved nine months later into the Notes from the Universe, but before I even got that far, a light went on in my head. I thought to myself, "Mike, wait a minute. It's been a couple of months now, and all you're doing is sending out free emails. Meanwhile, your life savings is getting smaller and smaller— better knock on some more doors!" (Good deduction, Sherlock Holmes.) Well, since I discovered that I really liked writing about life, dreams, and happiness, and I've always loved talking about these ideas with close friends and family, it dawned on me that one of the doors I should consider knocking on was professional speaking.

It wasn't that money alone was driving me, but I *did* have bills to pay, and there's nothing wrong with taking that practical aspect of life into account. So, given the absolute terror I had always harbored over public speaking, the door I knocked on was the one to a local Toastmasters club. (If you aren't familiar, Toastmasters is an organization that helps new speakers get a handle on their fear of public speaking and also helps good speakers become even better ones.)

After a few months of membership, I began entering competitions within the organization and reaching out to the real world as a speaker. Not that it was becoming easy; it wasn't, but I knew I had to "keep on keeping on" to assure I was in reach of life's magic. Based on advice I was given, I contacted local Rotary clubs, offering to be the guest speaker at one of their weekly meetings. (Rotary is a service and business networking organization with clubs in just about every city in every country on the planet, and *every* club hosts a guest speaker at each weekly meeting.) In Central Florida, over a year's time, I probably spoke at two dozen different clubs, giving my "Thoughts Become Things" speech. In that time, I also begin contacting Unity churches—very open-minded churches where my message was appreciated—offering to be a stand-in speaker whenever they needed one.

Before long, however, the light went on again, and I had to reassess my situation. I realized that now I was not only writing for free but I was also speaking for free! Time to knock on some more doors. I kept writing and speaking, but I also got excited about a new, incredible idea (or so I thought at the time): Survival Kits! Brilliant! I already had the Adventurers Club on the internet, and I figured my members would be anxious to buy something to support the Club while getting some fun stuff for themselves. The Kits would be for the "adventure of life!" with each Kit containing a cool T-shirt, a little book I had long ago self-published (the inventory of which was collecting dust in my garage), a key chain (also an unsold holdover from our former retailing days), and a certificate announcing the member's "initiation and good standing within the Club," signed by yours truly.

Indeed, it *was* a good idea, but my sales were limited to what my subscriber base would buy. After selling thirty Kits to a subscriber list of only several thousand at the time, I realized that my market was tapped out. With no more orders coming in, I thought, "Okay, it didn't happen the way I thought it would; knock on some more doors."

E-cards! I had discovered that some acquaintances were incorporating my poems (from our earlier T-shirt days) on their websites as free e-cards. On the e-card confirmation page that visitors saw after sending an e-card, there were banners advertising products and services, such as new credit cards, airline offers, and other specials, typically offered by big businesses. This was back in the days when advertisers were literally throwing money at internet advertising; it was the new frontier! Back then, if your website hosted an advertiser's banner, you could earn up to $10 to $25 *per click* when the people visiting your website were the ones doing the clicking! My friends were making $15,000 a month from the banners they were hosting on their e-card confirmation pages alone! *Whoo-hoo!*

I thought this was "meant to be." I had hundreds of poems from ten years in the T-shirt business. I could do my own e-cards! So I invested three months of working every day on creating my e-cards, and just as I was about to launch my own advertising banner blitz, the internet bubble burst, and those companies who had been throwing money at internet advertising vanished. For all my efforts, I never made more than $100 in any given month. Time to knock on some more doors.

The next door I knocked on belonged to the National Speakers Association. They had chapter meetings once a month in Lakeland, Florida, but they wouldn't let me join because I wasn't a professional. Instead, every month I happily paid a guest fee and sat in on their workshops, which are designed to help attendees hone their speaking skills and grow their speaking business. I also did some networking, talking to people who were professional speakers, and after a few months of attending these meetings, to my utter astonishment, a distinguished member invited me to create an audio program with him that we would release in hour-long installments one month at a time in the coming calendar year.

I was really excited. I came up with a title for our joint venture: *Infinite Possibilities: The Art of Living Your Dreams.* I remember thinking, "Clutch! Now that's a program *I* need to hear!"—given where my life was at the time. My partner taught me *everything* I needed to know about launching a new product online, from creating a sell-page to telling visitors about the benefits they'd receive if they at least tried the program.

On the day we debuted this audio program to each of our respective subscriber lists, I brought in $5,000, and my partner sold none. When he heard of my success, he congratulated me and bowed out. He said, "Mike, I can't split the proceeds with you in this program. Great job. It's all yours." Yikes! That meant I had two weeks to write, record, edit, master, and duplicate the first hour of *Infinite Possibilities*—alone. Uh-oh!

Hidden Miracles Revealed

Where would I get the content, the material—something that could live up to the promise of the title? *Aha!* My free talks! Wow, wasn't it a good thing I joined Toastmasters and created those speeches for Rotary and Unity churches? All I had to do was splice together a few speeches and the content for the first hour's script of *Infinite Possibilities* was done! I had already purchased a little hand-held digital recorder that I could use in my home office to create the audio master.

Then the question arose: how am I going to get paid my $5,000 from people all over the world who had already ordered this first installment? No problem. My survival kits experience had already enabled me to receive credit card payments online. In fact, I had already received *payment in full* for those first audio sales the night following the first promotional announcement!

Well, then how would I sell beyond this initial sales flurry? This was a concern because I had learned from my Survival Kits that my limited number of subscribers could only purchase a limited number of products. Where would I go to find new customers? No problem. I had learned all about affiliate, or viral, marketing from my e-cards and their banners, where the whole marketing idea was based on the concept that one person sent a card to their friends, who sent it to their friends, and so on, until you ended up with tens of thousands of people not only sending the card but seeing the confirmation page hosting the banners!

In fact, I went to the e-cards confirmation page on my website, which was still up and becoming very popular, and I removed the poorly performing banners for other businesses and replaced them all with new *Infinite Possibilities* banners! In the ensuing years, *Infinite Possibilities* became my business's bread and butter, and one of the internet's bestselling audio programs of all time.

In the year that led up to the release of *Infinite Possibilities*, it seemed to the *physical senses* that I encountered one humiliating failure after another. But what really happened was that at the beginning of that journey, in the *instant* I defined my end results of wealth and abundance, friends and laughter, international travel, and creative, fulfilling work, the Universe knew *exactly* how to get me there. Effectively, it worked backwards, calculating: "Okay, Mike, for you to have all these things, the shortest, quickest path will be for you to have an audio program that will be available to people all over the world via the internet. *But* the only way we can get you to have that audio program is to have content. Hey, let's get you past your fear of public speaking so that you're forced to create content, and as you get out into the world, more people can find you. Your credibility will be enhanced, and then you can start traveling internationally. Plus, we've got to get you credit card enabled."

And then, as I went out into the world knocking on doors, enabling this sequence of events to play out, it was as if I encountered one miracle after another, all clearly designed to bring me *Infinite Possibilities* and the life of my dreams as I had defined it—although again, with the physical senses alone; *I couldn't see any of this at the time.* Had I not had some understanding of the mechanics of manifestation and the magic of life, I would have been at risk of becoming discouraged, thinking that the Universe was trying to tell me, "Come on, Mike, can't you take a hint? You aren't cut out for your pie-in-the-sky dreams. Get real!" Though I have to admit, I had my moments of doubt; I faltered like anyone might have, and it was one very long year.

Wherever You Are, Know This

I don't know where you are in your life right now, but you might be feeling like you're stubbing your toes, that you're tripping, or that you're falling down. Do not interpret the journey with your physical senses alone. Instead, go within: know the truth. This system never fails, and every day, you get closer to your dreams. The Universe is metaphorically conspiring on your behalf, and just because you can't see this physically doesn't mean there's one moment or one door you've knocked on that will not be used by Divine Intelligence to bring you to the place you've been dreaming of. Don't quit because you can't see your progress, or because you feel like you're experiencing failure and sliding the other way. It's even possible that, for you *right now*, the tipping point toward your inevitable success has *already* been reached, although this can't yet be seen.

Never give up. Everything that's happened and is happening now is playing to your favor. Let this be your *modus operandi* and remember: throughout every journey, the miracles of progress are almost always invisible. What surrounds you today is no indicator of what's going to unfold tomorrow. *Where you are is never who you are.*

A NOTE FROM THE UNIVERSE

Three words to live by: Never trust appearances.

Of course, you can enjoy them all day long. Just don't trust them.

Trusting you,
The Universe

It Couldn't Be Easier

The greatest secret of the miraculous mechanics of manifestation is that the entire process happens in exactly the reverse order shown to us by our physical senses.

The starting point for all deliberate manifestations is always with the end result in mind. The end in mind forces the means—the physical logistics that will bring about its manifestation in the physical world; thought forces the circumstances. Our job is the easy part. It begins simply with deciding what you want! Instantly, universal principles then calculate and determine the entire sequence of events necessary to bring about whatever you've settled on, and this sequence will begin playing itself out as soon as you start physically moving in the general direction of whatever it is that you want. This is *exactly* how you've already been manifesting your entire life! How easy is that?

You Can Do This!

Here's an exercise that will help you rethink the actual sequence of events that brought about a life change for you. Use the following instructions to complete the chart on page 69 (or on a separate piece of paper) as you reconsider the experience. Once you understand—can *see*—how you've done what you've done, you can do it again and again. As they say, it's not magic to the magician.

Step One: *Turning Point:* Think of or jot down a major turning point that recently happened in your life but was unexpected, preferably a happy one, even though this exercise will work with any. It could be meeting somebody. It could be a so-called accident or coincidence. It could be a flash of insight. Just write down what you view to be a turning point in your life—perhaps spiritually, financially, romantically, or health-wise—in which everything changed. The turning point chosen shouldn't be so old that you don't remember some of the circumstances that brought you to it.

Step Two: *Life Circumstances:* Now think of or jot down the factors you encountered that put you in a place to later experience the main turning point. It could be your mood; mind-set; circumstances; or what happened in the days, weeks, and months leading up to this turning point that made it possible for you to be in the right place at the right time. It could be anything, like sitting next to somebody who told you about a great book, informed you about an upcoming conference, or offered you a job—whatever. Name the experiences you had that *physically* put you in a place that enabled this major life turning point.

Step Three: *Life Changes:* Now think of or jot down the main areas of your life that were affected by the turning point. Was it your happiness, your abundance levels, your career? Be specific.

Now, there are two ways of viewing this exercise and the sequence of events that unfolded from your turning point experience. The conventional way would be on a timeline. In story form, it might sound like, "I was flying to New York to

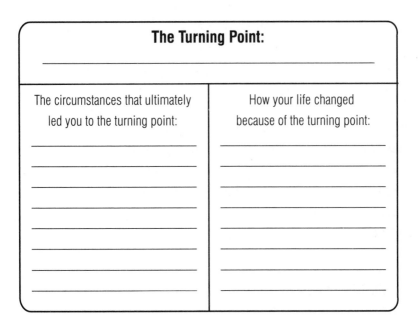

The Turning Point:

_____

The circumstances that ultimately led you to the turning point:	How your life changed because of the turning point:
_____	_____
_____	_____
_____	_____
_____	_____
_____	_____
_____	_____
_____	_____

see my grandmother, who had suddenly called me out of the blue and offered to pay for my Manhattan vacation. Anyway, because I'd just seen this new commercial on television for X Airlines offering double flying miles for domestic trips, I decided to fly X Airlines. Coincidentally, I sat next to this guy, and all he could talk about was the new Dan Brown book.

"The next thing you know, I'm in New York City, and the subway train I'd normally take is out of order, so I had to walk to the next stop. On my way, I pass this bookstore, and because I was just told about the new Dan Brown book, I go in to see if they have any copies left. Sure enough, they're sold out. But when I was walking out of the store, another book caught my eye. It was called _Manifesting Change_. Something drew me to it, and within a few minutes I had my own copy. Ever since then, my life has changed; I have a new relationship, a new job, and I've never been more photogenic!"

This narration captures the sequence of events as experienced by our physical senses on a timeline (see diagram A below). And if we liked the results of the change they led to, we'd then logically think that creating more changes like it requires being really lucky (giving away our power) or wrangling events (messing with the *cursed hows*, also giving away our power) in order to meet someone else recommending a book, thereby leading us on an unpredictable goose chase. We may even tell the Universe that we want all of this to happen by December 31st so that we can start off the new year in style!

Diagram A

Life Circumstances ⟶ Turning Point ⟶ Life Changes

◄─────────── **Experienced on Timeline** ───────────►

In actuality, what really happened, and the second way to view this sequence of events, is that they were "assembled" in exactly the reverse order of what happened on the linear timeline. Kicking things off, somewhere along the way, you began *redefining* whatever you named in the *Life Changes* portion of this exercise. I don't know if it was happiness or health or credit card debt, but *you saw it in a new light*. You wanted more, or less, of it. You thought of your would-be life as if this change had already taken place.

You created a new expectation. You stopped settling for less, *and your behavior changed as well*. The Universe—life's metaphysical principles—responded, instantly determining the ideal sequence of events that could bring about the life change, including a necessary turning point and what would bring you to it. It worked *backwards* from your new vision or end results to sew together events, circumstances, and people who would be in the right place at the right time to merge your *physical now* with this *envisioned now* (see diagram B).

Diagram B

Life Changes ⟶ Turning Point ⟶ Life Circumstances

← Assembled and Calculated Beyond Time and Space →

Once you realize that *this* was how the sequence of events was orchestrated to bring about your changed levels of happiness or abundance (or whatever your end result), then you know how to do it again, *deliberately*. Right? Our part is the easy part! To repeat the pattern, go back within and redefine your life with the changes you'd like to experience. Imagine the changes *already* done. Settle for nothing less and *behave* as if you knew your success was inevitable. The Universe will grab the baton and realize the kind of turning points you need, the kind of inspiration, the kind of friends or clients, the kind of circumstances, and it'll begin rearranging and programming the days, weeks, and months preceding that turning point to set you up for the ultimate change you envisioned. This is how the mechanics really work. And to restate the obvious, the only other thing required of you is that you show up, taking action in the general direction of your dreams so that you can meet with "accidents" and "serendipities" that will allow the Universe's plan to unfold without a hitch.

A Note from the Universe

*It's not possible. For better or worse, you cannot significantly
change your life by manipulating the material world—
not by working harder, not by studying longer,
not by schmoozing, not by sweating, not by fasting,
not by the hair of your chinny chin chin!*

*But change—great change—is inescapable . . .
when you first begin manipulating the world of your thoughts.*

*It is that simple.
The Universe*

4

Playing the Matrix

ma·trix: something within or from which something else originates, develops, or takes form; resembling a mathematical matrix especially in rectangular arrangement of elements into rows and columns

~MERRIAM-WEBSTER

Why a Matrix?

The Matrix I created came about after a massive struggle on my part to literally invent an entirely new way of seeing and understanding the *effects* of where we focus our energy (something [our focus] from which something else [the consequences of our focus] originates). After weeks of dwelling on my desired end result and countless attempts to explain it in terms anyone would understand (moving in its general direction), I suddenly noticed loosely drafted words that unintentionally appeared as columns in my handwritten notes, and from which I had drawn arrows indicating certain ideal, and less than ideal, consequences. Upon my discovery, I seized the opportunity to encase and expand upon these makeshift columns, which resulted in a very simple rectangular arrangement resembling a mathematical matrix. And its clarity and usefulness since have been stunning. I shared it with more than 10,000 people at live events during my second world tour, and it became apparent that this Matrix is as revolutionary and exciting for others as it has been for me.

Basically, playing the Matrix is about achieving clarity and gaining understanding of what it is you *really* want. This sounds as though it should be a very simple task, but being raised in a society that encourages us to mess with the *cursed hows* and place undo emphasis on details that don't really matter, we often unwittingly mix and match what we really want with ideas of how to get it or the details it promises. Causing further confusion are the many sound bites taken from different teachers on the subject of deliberate manifestation, which seemingly, or in actuality, create contradictions. I've seen myself get bogged down over choosing my end results (the most memorable time, "coincidentally," was just as I was about to create this material).

What's a Good End Result?

My mother and brother often come over to my house, sometimes with the sole purpose of having a "powwow," to get excited about life and share readings from books we've discovered or insights we've garnered on our own. On one of these visits, Andy wanted to talk us through a guided visualization he'd just created.

"OK, you guys. Relax. Breathe deep. Inhale . . . Exhale . . . Now close your eyes," Andy began. Then he went to his boom box and cranked up the music from *Chariots of Fire*. "Now I want you to imagine you're running along the beach at sunrise; the waves are crashing, and you're exploding with an overwhelming feeling of *gratitude*."

I'm a good sport, so I'm following along, running down the beach and exploding with gratitude, when a voice in my head asks, "Mike, what are you grateful for?" (*Not that you have to have something in particular to be grateful for*; just feeling gratitude is enough. But I decided to answer this voice.) It came to me right away that I wanted to be grateful for that perfect relationship. Oh my gosh!

So, I'm jogging down the beach, and I'm so happy. Looking to my side, I see that *she's* right there jogging beside me! I'm beaming gratitude, and she is too; even the cadence of our running matches. All is well as the sun begins rising until the same voice asks, "Mike, are you sure you want to *force* a relationship? Relationships have always taken care of themselves for you. You don't have to *make* something happen. Just live your life, dance life's dance; and when you're ready and the right person's ready, it will happen effortlessly." And so I think to myself, *Yeah, maybe there's something to that.*

Andy's still guiding us down the beach, but now I feel a little lonely, which is when the voice returns yet again, "Come on. Give me something to be grateful for!"

OK, I got it! A red Ferrari! Wow! It's glistening in the sun on the beach right now, and as I run past it, I admire its deft lines, its sleek curves, its immaculate paint; I'm just beaming with gratitude . . . when I hear, "Mike, if you were to manifest a yellow Lamborghini, would you be devastated because you didn't get your red Ferrari?" Why, no. No, I wouldn't! I'd be pretty delighted with a yellow Lamborghini.

"Well, then why are you thinking about a red Ferrari? You're just closing the door on a yellow Lamborghini. Be a little more general, not so specific. Leave room for *something even better.*"

Right! Something even better! Yeah, just forget the car thing and let me think of something else . . .

Andy's still talking, walking us through gratitude, and I have a new bright idea: a fabulous house on the ocean! As I'm running past this imaginary mansion, I wave to the MTV *Cribs* crew, who is filming my "crib" for their version of *Architectural Digest of the Stars.* The place is packed, the music is pumping, and the people are pointing and waving back *at me*! "There's Mike! The owner! He's so cool!" I'm feeling *so* much gratitude now . . . until, "Mike, is this all about the bling? Is it going to take material things for you to feel gratitude?" And so I somewhat sheepishly back away from that image, feeling a little bit embarrassed. *Yeah. Don't go there. Think of something else.*

I decide to be grateful for getting to write the Notes from the Universe, which at the time were being sent to about 100,000 people daily. I imagine them bouncing off websites and servers all over the planet. *Millions upon millions* of people are receiving their daily Note from the Universe. I'm just so happy and grateful for my role in their creation and the joy they bring to others . . . until I hear that pesky voice again: "Mike, maybe the way you could reach the *most* people isn't through email. Maybe it'll be a book. Or a blog. Maybe it'll be your next world tour, perhaps a *stadium* tour! Who knows? But if you're focusing on one thing—the Notes—you're actually excluding other possibilities."

I'm about to go crazy. I decide that I'm just going to think about the Adventurers Club, which is my umbrella organization that encompasses everything I'm now doing career-wise— when Andy suddenly says, "Okay. That's it. Nice job!" *I wanted to kill him.* I'm literally perspiring from this exhausting mental run down the beach, feeling that it was a complete waste of time for me. I was unable to focus on a single thing without some form of guilt, admonishment, or self-criticism! *Why was it so painfully difficult?*

Again, it's because there are so many different schools of thought on the subject. Should you think of the details? Or should you be general and allow the Universe to bring you something even better than what you're capable of imagining? What about other people, as in relationships? Don't they have a say in how their life unfolds? What about the bling? Can we be too materialistic? Even though *every single thing I had thought about in gratitude was fair and reasonable* (there was nothing wrong with any of them being an end result), I was still stuck and mired in confusion from the doubts, ambiguities, societal pressures, and contradictory thoughts that were running through my head. This is when I had my epiphany for *the need to help others on the topic, as much as myself,* to get clear in their thoughts and end results for how they dreamed of changing their life.

Overview

The Matrix, as you'll see in the following figure, includes six columns in its lower half that represent the entire spectrum of reality as we know it—all possible dreams or end results. These columns are the heart of the Matrix: they encompass anything and everything a human being could desire. The Matrix is like an artist's color palette, except that it offers a palette of end results to choose from.

Let's look at each of the six columns, one at a time, beginning with the far left. In the two left-hand columns, the

The Matrix
©Mike Dooley

The Entire Spectrum of Reality; Containing All Possible Dreams/End Results →

Thought & Emotion	The Illusions—Dependent on Time, Space, Matter, or Others			
	Physical—Generalized	Physical—Type 1	Physical—Type 2	Physical—Type 3
Ethereal Highest and Best End Results	Excellent!	Narrower yet reasonable. Begins limiting options.	Significantly Dependent upon Others or aligned beliefs.	Entirely dependent upon Others. Worst-case *cursed hows*.
Dependent Solely Upon You	Dependent upon the Illusions.	Increasingly dependent on the Illusions and upon Others.		Entirely dependent upon Others.
Happiness	Understanding Gratitude Spirituality Confidence Creativity Acceptance Tolerance Compassion Patience Self-Love Etc.	**The Fantastic 5** Livelihood Abundance Health Relationships Appearance	Possessions Career/Work Wealth Levels Friends Associates Family Harmony Fun and Games Hobbies Fitness Talents Etc.	Projects Events Diet Investments Timelines Type of Car $ Amounts Etc.	Specific People Specific Employer Specific Customer Specific Client Specific Stock Specific Plans Specific House Etc.

← Attach! Attach! Attach! →   ← Detach! Detach! Detach! →

← Circumstances (The Universe Manages) →   ← Cursed Hows (All on You!) →

possible end results are ethereal, or intangible (see the top half of the chart). These end results are thought- or emotion-based qualities, and their manifestation, or achievement, is *entirely dependent upon us*, our perspectives, and our state of mind. All of the columns to their right, however, include end results that are *dependent upon the Illusions*, meaning that their manifestation relies upon time, space, matter, or other people. As we move to the right across the Matrix, each new column includes manifestations that are increasingly dependent upon other people, their thoughts, and their manifestations.

Thought- and Emotion-Based End Results

Column 1: This is the happiness column. You've heard it before a million times: *happiness is an inside job*; our thoughts are entirely dependent on us.

Column 2: Beginning with understanding, this column simply illustrates that there are other possible end results, besides happiness, that are solely dependent upon us. Like happiness, these desired thought- or emotion-based objectives are inside jobs.

Illusion-Based End Results

Column 3: Beginning with livelihood, I call these the Fantastic 5. Even though they're dependent upon the Illusions, they're stated generally, leaving fantastic latitude for *how* they may manifest into our lives. The Fantastic 5 contain anything and everything within the *physical world* that you might want to change in your life, yet stated in a *general* sense. This is thefirst column that "dips its toes" into the Illusions. That's huge—a big leap. End results chosen from the first two columns are solely dependent upon us; they're ethereal, whereas now we're moving into desires for change that are dependent upon time, space, matter, and, in a general sense, other people. Are your antennae up? Think this is problematic? Hardly!

We are the otters of the Universe—joyful, fun-loving matter manipulators by birth. We are the gladiators of eternity who created this bastion of perfection in the cosmos. Playing in matter is our prerogative (not to mention a compelling reason all on its own) to be alive in the jungles of time and space. We ourselves, *physically speaking*, are matter-breathing beings!

Matter is not intrinsically a bad thing, nor is it bad to want to have it in your life in ways that please you. Illusion-based desires for change are perfectly acceptable, *especially when generally stated*. If you want abundance or a change in your livelihood, those are such general wishes that there's almost infinite freedom given to metaphysical principles to fit their bill and give you what you're asking for (and if you don't understand the importance of this yet, you will soon).

Let's take another look over each of the Fantastic 5 so that there are no questions in your mind as to what they represent.

Livelihood: This refers to how you actively fill your days, whether you work, volunteer, stay at home, or raise children.

Abundance: This refers to material abundance. You could, of course, apply the concept of abundance to anything—friends, hobbies, or love—but in this instance, make no mistake, we are taking about the bucks!

Health: This refers to your physical body.

Relationships: Hmmm—you could say this refers to someone else's physical body! Whether friends, clients, customers, life partners, or lovers.

Appearance: This refers to being pleased with your physical appearance. It's primarily for those people who want to lose weight, gain weight, or otherwise change how they look.

Columns 4 & 5: Physical—Type 1 and Physical—Type 2 are purely arbitrary names I've chosen to help with some distinctions. Even the examples I give are somewhat arbitrary, and in some cases the column they belong to could be debated, yet what I've attempted to illustrate is that the more we move to the right, the more dependent our manifestations become on *specific* details and circumstances, and moreover, upon *specific* people. The more we move to the right, the more specific our desires are.

In Physical—Type 1, we're talking about material possessions but still somewhat generally; we're talking about wealth levels. We're also talking about family harmony and friendships.

And then in Physical—Type 2, we are getting into more specific investments, circumstances, projects, timelines, and dollar amounts.

Column 6: Physical—Type 3, the last column on the Matrix, is on the opposite end of the spectrum that started with the happiness column. When we choose end results from this column, not only are we hinging our success in manifesting change upon the illusions, but we're also hinging it on specific people and their choices: the *worst-case of the cursed hows!* Such end results are implying that you're not going to get what you want—your desired life changes—until *a certain someone* changes. It's like saying, "Look, I'm not going to be happy until you shape up . . . until you give me a raise . . . until you show me respect . . . or until you sell me my dream home, which you presently have the audacity to call your own!" Horror of horrors! This is when we totally give away our power.

Playing the Matrix

Metaphysically Speaking

The Matrix is essentially a tool that reveals where we should place our focus within the entire spectrum of reality to trigger and bring about certain results or consequences. It helps us choose end results in a way that maximizes our power and ensures success. It reveals what we can, and in some cases *must*, delegate to universal principles, or life's magic, as opposed to sweating it out ourselves. And it reveals exactly what we can't and should never delegate to the Universe.

It demonstrates that there's actually a flow to all manifestations and that there may or may not be consequences to what we choose. A flow that when harnessed, sweeps us along almost effortlessly, and when ignored can leave us feeling like we're fighting against the entire Universe. When "played" properly, the Matrix gives us a shortcut to manifesting the most fulfilling and rewarding life possible.

So, how do you "play" the Matrix? Well, where did we say change begins when we talked about the miraculous mechanics of manifestation? We said it begins with the end *in mind*—the end result. *It begins with thought.* And we said that thought forces the physical circumstances necessary for there to be a corresponding manifestation in our life. This tips us off that we should begin playing this Matrix *on the left-hand side*!

By playing the Matrix from the left, the *necessary* consequences to the right assemble themselves in perfect ways to yield our desires. This flow from left to right is key. From whatever column you choose to manifest change, anything to the right *necessary for its manifestation* will be flushed out and arranged so that you can have it. This is "the end in mind" forcing the details and circumstances that will bring it to pass as a manifestation.

The farther to the left you start, the more you delegate from the right to the Universe to arrange. The farther you start to the right, the less you delegate simply because there's less of the Matrix left! Furthermore, only the directly related items to the right of your choice will be affected.

For instance, let's say you want more abundance in your life from column three, which is an excellent end result. Only the relevant items in the columns to the right of abundance, *which need to be organized or forced in order for you to have abundance*, will be taken care of by the mechanics of manifestation, and no more.

So, with abundance as our starting point, what to the right of abundance must be forced in order for you to experience its manifestation? Material possessions? Check. Career and/or work? Not necessarily. You might find abundance in a way other than your career and work, so you may remain unhappy there. Wealth levels? Check. Friends? No connection. Having abundance does not mean you will have friends. Family harmony? No connection.

As you move across the spectrum to the right, away from abundance, only those things necessary for having abundance in your life will be forced in perfect ways for you, but nothing else. So again, the farther over that you start the process on the left-hand side of the Matrix, the more you leave to the Universe to organize for you on the right. Happiness, therefore, which is the farthest to the left, is the ultimate end result because *everything* is to the right of it—meaning you are giving life's mechanics *free reign to arrange all of the hows and details.*

Happiness is the ultimate end result because the Universe, being an extension of yourself, knows that the only way you can be truly happy is if you've got abundance, health, friends, harmony in your relationships, and joyful satisfaction with how you look. In order for happiness to be made manifest, it requires that *everything* to the right of happiness, including each of the Fantastic 5 categories, will be taken care of for you *once you take action in its general direction.* The only thing that cannot be forced when happiness is your end result is *specific* people in the farthest right-hand column, because people get to make up their own mind as to what thoughts they're going to think and what world they're going to create. This isn't to say that you can't influence them if your wishes are in alignment with theirs. If your wishes don't match, however, and as long as you aren't insisting that these people be in your life, *others who are in alignment with you will begin appearing.*

Happiness is the ultimate end result, but I know what it's like: at first glance, you might have that inner sinking feeling, "Yeah, but what if that's all I get?! What if I just get happy but remain broke, sick, or lonely!" Not possible! You simply cannot be *truly* happy if you are broke, sick, or lonely. If you focus on deep, true happiness and follow through with taking action using the suggestions given and those still to come, then everything else in your life will take care of itself so that this ethereal emotion can be experienced—made manifest—in the jungles of time and space. If happiness is what you're dwelling on, then the only way it can truly happen is if the entirety of your life comes together in perfectly harmonious ways.

Still, because you're a matter manipulator, a playful otter of the Universe, by all means, go to the third column and give extra special attention to anything in the Fantastic 5 that you want. Just understand, however, if you're giving something in the third column your exclusive attention, it will not have any effect on the other areas of your life that needn't be forced in order for you to experience its manifestation. Nor, as we're about to review, will it necessarily add to your happiness, because the Matrix doesn't flow from right to left!

Old School

Where do you think most people begin playing the Matrix when it comes to manifesting change in their life? Yup, on the right-hand side! In fact, in most cases, people begin playing the Matrix *in the last column on the right-hand side*, Physical—Type 3, and their entire life approach to manifesting change begins with trying to change other people! Every hope they have is hinged on someone else's behavior, because they think that if everyone else changes, *then* their life is going to blast off. *Then* they're going to find the right job, the right investments, and the right circumstances; everything will be easier at home and at work; they'll fall into abundance; and, ultimately, they'll be happy.

But the Matrix does not flow from right to left! *Things do not become thoughts; thoughts become things!* These people have got the entire equation backwards. It's like putting all of your eggs in one basket except it's worse: the basket doesn't even belong to you! Not only are you very unlikely to meet with any consistent success, but even if you do convince others to behave as you wish, it'll do nothing for you on the left side of the Matrix. It will not ensure your happiness, fulfillment, confidence, or anything else. So what if Rocko starts sending you flowers more often? What's that going to do for your health, your career, your clarity, your appearance, or your overall life happiness? Nothing!

You might even get your employer to give you a raise, but if you haven't been focusing on abundance or happiness, it's very likely that the raise will come in one door and go straight out the other. "Coincidentally," the car will need a repair, the roof will start leaking, or your rent will increase.

Grasping that there's a flow to the Matrix is all-important. That's why, in the very bottom row to the left, it says "Circumstances (The Universe Manages)," which means that when you start playing the Matrix on the left-hand side, the Universe manages the circumstances—the *hows*—that will bring about the manifestation. Everything to the right of your choice *that is necessary for its manifestation* will be arranged for you in the most harmonious way possible, and you'll finally witness just how powerful you truly are. Whereas if you start on the right side of the Matrix in order to manifest major life changes, the bottom row says, "*Cursed Hows* (All on You!)." This means you're setting out to create change by beginning with the illusions because you mistakenly think that by physically rearranging the props on your stage, you'll eventually achieve greater and greater objectives, and ultimately generate happiness. Yet any success achieved this way will only ever be fleeting.

The Matrix versus Conventional Wisdom

Vision Boards and Scrapbooks

As mentioned, I've already delivered this material all over the world, so I well understand how much of it may *seem* to contradict the commonly accepted ideas already associated with deliberately manifesting change. A lady in Texas asked, "Mike, at home I have a vision board filled with pictures of things you'd find in the right three columns of your Matrix. Am I playing the Matrix backwards?" Not necessarily.

I have a vision board at home too, and for twenty years I've worked with scrapbooks. Both are essentially places to paste pictures and quotes that inspire me and help me to *think thoughts* of my dreamed-of life. They're fabulous tools.

The great usefulness of vision boards (and/or scrapbooks) comes from how you view what you're looking at. If you see the pictures as the be-all and end-all of your happiness—if you're *attached* to the "things" pictured, wanting exactly *that* car or *that* specific home on a cliff—then you're messing with the *cursed hows*. *Attachment* to the details is what creates problems.

However, I think we instinctively know not to use a vision board that way. A vision board should be used to ramp up the energy and the excitement one feels about the *bigger, grander* life view that includes overall happiness, overall abundance, and overall harmony. The specifics on the vision board should *not* be all-important in themselves; they're just reminders of the fuller life you're really after—trinkets, if you will, or the icing on a much bigger cake. If that's how you use your vision board or your scrapbook, then more power to you. You are not playing the Matrix incorrectly.

Realize that *nothing* you could put on your vision board compares to the big picture of happiness—not even any one of the Fantastic 5 generalities. A new car, no matter how exotic, doesn't compare to possessing abundance. A mocked up photo of you sitting with Oprah on her television show does not compare to having a rewarding, fulfilling career. A picture capturing a moment you shared with laughing and smiling people does not compare to having true, solid friendships. These images pale in comparison to what they could and *should* imply as representations of your grander life. The grander life is what's of paramount importance; the subsequent details, or consequences, of possessing that grander life will take care of themselves, and the right car, home, circle of friends, and career will show up as they are forced into place by the larger, universal vision (coupled with the action you take in their direction).

I'm not saying don't imagine details; I'm saying *do not attach to them*! It's entirely *how* you view those images on your vision board or scrapbook that will determine whether or not you're properly playing the Matrix.

Never Attach to the Outcome!

The second question that's been raised among my audience members (and may be in your head right now) is tied to the commonly heard advice that says, "Never attach to the out-come!" In other words, *never attach to the end result.* Have you ever heard that before? I'm sure you have, and it's actually good advice, but it seems to be diametrically opposed to everything I've just told you about beginning with an end result.

Let me ask you: what are most people's end results? What are the outcomes in life that most people attach to? Yes! Items on the right side of the Matrix! Most people's outcomes or end results involve specific people or are significantly dependent upon time, space, or certain material things. And because that's where most people focus when it comes to end results and outcomes, the advice is wise indeed: do not attach to end results or outcomes.

But with what we've covered already in this chapter, if people begin understanding that their end results should always be general—ideally happiness, but no more refined than abundance, livelihood, health, relationships, or appearance—then *attach, attach, attach*! How else could you expect there to be change unless you focus on it, insist upon it, attach to it, and move with it? As natural-born creators, it's our obligation and responsibility to choose what we want for our lives *but in general terms*, without limiting ourselves and universal principles by insisting on unimportant details or *cursed hows.*

Helping Others

Now let me add one more point of clarification: the six columns of the Matrix reveal *anything and everything from the entire spectrum of reality* that you could choose for desired change. It includes, *and you could choose,* your boss giving you a raise *and* your child's happiness. I haven't said you couldn't choose whatever you want, even from the far right column, but I want you to understand how the Matrix flows—how manifestations can or cannot affect other dreams and end results. I want you to understand what happens when you push certain buttons (where you place your attention) and what the likely consequences may or may not be.

If you're visualizing your own happiness, everything else in your life will take care of itself as you physically move with and toward happiness. If, however, you're wishing for little Johnny's happiness, there *will* be limits to what *you* can achieve because little Johnny will have his own agenda, wishes, desires, ambitions, thoughts, and beliefs. And should you even succeed, if this were your *only* life objective, your own happiness may be completely unaffected. This, incidentally, doesn't mean that you shouldn't try to help your children find their place (with your thoughts and other efforts) or that you can't be very influential. Moreover, the example of wanting to positively influence your own children is far removed from trying to influence other people to serve your end results.

Nevertheless, by visualizing someone else's happiness, no matter who they are, you will help them *if and only if they are open to receiving help.* Good thoughts for anyone will be received and understood. In a sense, it's like sending a love note, so go for it. Just understand that whether or not they open that love note, and whether or not they choose to react to that love note in a positive way, is entirely up to them. In this regard, when you have desires for someone else, you don't want to attach your happiness to the manifestation of those desires.

You Can Do This!

Here's a simple little exercise that will help you better understand the distinction and importance between your generalized and detailed desires. Using the work area on page 92, choose a Fantastic 5 area of your life that you'd like to change. Then make a list of the happy consequences and details you'd experience from successfully bringing about this change.

By the way, I've heard from some in my audiences that "consequences" is a loaded word with negative connotations. This is *not* my intent. I'm using it to mean the *byproducts* of change. We're going to use the right side of the table to define your life in terms of the consequences that come from successfully creating the Fantastic 5 category change listed. This is where you can put in loads of details, and *details are good!* The details are *awesome* for getting emotionally excited about the big-picture life changes you desire; we just don't want to attach to them, or worse, unwittingly swap them for the big-picture change.

In the right column, also list how you'll feel about the accomplishment, as well as all of the material "things" you'd then have in your life once you've successfully manifested change in the listed category. Make the list of details at least a dozen points long, and if you're getting carried away with the fun, make it much longer (using your own paper or the back of this book).

With this exercise, I wanted to achieve three things. First, I wanted you to discern the difference between being general and being detailed, and have an understanding of what I mean when I say "consequences." They always come about *after* you manifest the larger, more general change that you set out to manifest. They are never connected to *how* you bring about the change, nor do they include details of its acquisition. Go *beyond* the change and imagine how your life will be *after* you already have the abundance, the new relationship, the svelte physique, or whatever it is you chose at the start of this exercise. I wanted you to really get into that world of your end result, as if the changes had already happened.

Getting into the Details Exercise

Fantastic 5 Category	Consequences and details that will come from successful change:

The second thing I wanted to demonstrate is that it is *from* the general, big-picture end result that the details and consequences *flow*. The loose generality gives rise to innumerable possibilities as far as the consequences go. You could probably extend your list to many more pages, especially considering that some of your details could then make possible even more details. And this flow, from the big picture to the details, is mirrored in the flow of all time-space manifestations, not just revealing that the generality makes the details possible, but also reflecting that *the flow does not work in reverse.*

For instance, if you began the exercise by first listing details like owning a Ferrari, a boat, and a condo in Hawaii, such details in and of themselves do not automatically mean you're truly wealthy, as each could either come with its own debts attached or these items could perhaps be your *only* possessions! Moreover, without the clarity that true financial abundance is what you're really after (if that was the category you chose), it may never actually be considered and focused upon if you are not explicitly stating so.

Third and finally, I wanted to illustrate that vast difference in importance between the general category versus its consequences and details. Correct me if I'm wrong, but the thing that really matters most to you is changing that big, general area of your life, right? Not one of the consequences or details even comes close to being as important to you. Can you see this distinction? I bet that when you look at your list in this exercise, you could probably tear off and trash an entire page of details and replace it with another list of details that would be equally satisfying to you. Until now, however, most people, upon learning of their manifesting powers, almost immediately latch onto a specific car, diet, home, or job; lose their focus on the big picture; and give their power away to other people, mistakenly thinking that if they have enough little successes, the big picture will take care of itself. Yet, if one never gives the big picture any attention or thought, the approach is almost doomed at the outset.

Getting into the Details

For reasons that are now obvious, I've spent the entirety of this chapter moving your attention away from unimportant details and toward realizing the all-important concept of focusing on big-picture change. If I've succeeded, I've perhaps created a new, albeit temporary, challenge: how does one get excited about something as seemingly vague as more happiness, greater abundance, or being pleased with your physical appearance?

And the answer is, by *getting into the details*, or the consequences as just defined, that will result from your pending success in the general life category. As I deliberately stated during the last exercise, *the details are good*! The details give clarity and enhance focus. They literally help you taste, touch, hear, smell, or feel exactly what the big-picture generality promises. The difference, from now on, is that we will no longer attach or insist upon them.

So now that we've sorted out what's important and what's not, and I've shown you why to stay general and how to get into the details of your general success, let's use those details to *imagine* your anticipated big-picture success. Using your imagination as a tool toward making your dreams come true should be an absolute no-brainer when you understand that *thoughts becoming things* is the absolute be-all and end-all of how time and space are assembled. This leads to the realization that visualizing, as an exercise, is perhaps the very least you can do to bring about the very most in terms of fantastic life changes, no matter how "woo-woo" that may sound.

Visualizing the details can be approached exactly as I described using vision boards and scrapbooks. Just as the photographs of those tools are not what the exercise is really about, neither are the images in your mind. The point and purpose behind staring at the photographs or visualizing them in your head is to get you excited about *the big picture*—your grander, fuller, more rewarding life. As long as you're not attaching to the details or turning them into end results of their own, visualizing simply creates a mold that the elements of time and space rush to fill with the right details, which will find you at the right time in the most harmonious way as you move in the general direction of your big-picture dreams.

Creative Visualization Guidelines

Here are the six visualizing guidelines that I personally follow when I use visualization to get into the details; they're not rules. You can come up with your own, and develop your own patterns and habits. For me, these are what work, and there is some rationale behind each that I'll share, but I'm always making exceptions to them and so can you. This exercise is simply based upon *thoughts becoming things*, which is really the only "rule" there is.

1. Visualize once a day.

Once a day is all that's necessary. Of course, you can think happy thoughts on your way to work or while falling asleep at night, and you might even visualize a second or third time every now and then. But overall, let this be an exercise that you do one time each day, and then let it go.

I've met too many people who've never visualized before, yet upon reading or hearing about visualization, they suddenly get very excited, and then want to do it forty-seven times a day! If you go overboard, thinking that if once is good a hundred times must be better, chances are you're going to start comparing your dreamed-of champagne and caviar life with where you now are, and become overwhelmed with the disparity and distance that it seems you'll have to travel. You may even become discouraged to the point of quitting visualization altogether. Moreover, if you do it too often, you'll be constantly living in some future world, missing out on who you already are and all you already have. Don't do that to yourself. Visualize once a day and let it go.

2. Visualize no longer than five to ten minutes at a time.

If you try to visualize longer, no matter who you are, you're going to start daydreaming—probably about sex or something equally distracting! And then you're going to get mad at yourself. You'll label yourself, thinking you must have adult ADD, then draw the false conclusion that visualizing doesn't work for you. *It does work for you* and it's easy; just limit yourself to no more than five or ten minutes. I visualize every morning before work for just four minutes.

3. Imagine every conceivable detail.

Playfully create imaginative, elaborate scenes in your mind's eye that depict your changed life. Imagine the sights, sounds, colors, textures, and aromas. Make the image in your mind as real and vivid as possible. Of course, I'm *not* talking about attaching to those details, insisting that *they* are what flood into your life. Just use them to get excited about all the amazing changes you will soon be experiencing. This is how the details are valuable—even priceless.

4. Feel the emotion.

Feel what you'd expect to feel, experiencing the life you dream of having. Feel the joy, the confidence, the satisfaction. No matter how silly it seems when you're shouting "whoo-hoo-hoo-hoo" in that dark and quiet room, do it! How badly do you want what you want? Chances are that you want it bad enough to get a little "stupid" when you're visualizing in the privacy of your own home.

Emotion is the turbocharger of change; our emotions super-charge the thoughts associated with them. This extra charge overpowers your other competing (or sometimes contradictory) thoughts, drawing circumstances into your path that facilitate your big dream's manifestation. I tell anybody who wants to bring about major life changes that they should begin with a visualization program; however, I tell anyone who wants to bring major life changes *quickly* to visualize *with emotion*.

As a side note, many of my audience members have told me that they aren't able to imagine details. They tell me their mind doesn't go there, and they even wonder what it is every-one else is seeing. If this is you, perhaps you're actually at an advantage because the most important "things" anyone can put in their mental imagery are not the physical details but the emotional ones. Drop all of the physical details and just feel the joy, which truly cuts to the chase, bypassing all *cursed hows* and giving the Universe maximum latitude to work out the details that will bring that smile to your face—*the way you put it out there when you visualized.*

5. Put yourself in the picture.

You've got to be there, in the picture, if you want your manifestation to include you. For example, let's just say one of the details you're visualizing is a new car. Right before you close your eyes, look at the back of your hands. Your hands are different from anybody else's: your fingers, nails, hairs, wrinkles, and even the rings you wear are unique. In your mind's eye, visualize *your hands* wrapping around the steering wheel of whatever it is that you most want to be driving.

This was confirmed beyond a doubt by a woman who wrote me and said, "Mike, I'm having trouble visualizing. I want that new Volkswagen Beetle, retro design, sapphire blue!" And of course I replied to her that this is not asking the Universe for too much; there are a lot of these cars out there. Visualizing shouldn't be hard.

"Mike, you don't understand. I was recently involved in a traffic accident." ("Uh-oh," I thought.) "I was rear-ended," she continued, "by a sapphire blue Volkswagen Beetle with a retro design." Ah-ha! "And, Mike, that's just the half it. This morning. . . ." (I could almost hear her crying between the words) "I watched my neighbor drive to work in her brand new, sapphire blue, retro-design Volkswagen Beetle!"

The moral of this story? Put *yourself* in the picture. And for that matter, while we're at it, include happy, smiling pictures of yourself on your vision board and scrapbook! Visualizing is done to improve *your* life—be there!

Feel your toes in the sand at the beach, or feel your hand in the palm of another as you walk together on a moonlit night. Smell the aromas of the scene you're imagining, perhaps the salt in the air or the smoke from the fireplace. And of course, feel the joy. Happiness is what you're really after. Plus, emotions automatically put you in the picture.

6. Dwell from the end result—or beyond.

This is just one more way to say what I've already said many times: do not mess with the *cursed hows*. When visualizing, go to the finished picture, where your dream has *already* come true. Do not visualize *how* it will come true! The *cursed hows* are the bane of our primitive existence. We've all been told since we could understand words that we *should* mess with the *hows*—that we're irresponsible and reckless if we don't. The truth of the matter, however, is that messing with the *hows* is *what slows us down,* tying the hands of the Universe and leading us to think that we must carry the weight of the world upon our shoulders.

Incidentally, should you be wondering how it's possible to "move in the general direction of your dreams" while not messing with the *cursed hows*, this is addressed specifically in chapter 5. For now, we're talking about visualizing, and when you do this, don't even *think* about thinking about *anything else.*

A NOTE FROM THE UNIVERSE

Did you know that whenever you think a brand new thought, however fleeting, there are switches flicked here? Buttons pressed? Levers thrown? Banners unfurled? Wheels turned? Hats tipped? Winks winked? Angels sent? Connections made and conga lines formed?

For starters.

*You wouldn't even believe me if I told you
what happens when you visualize.*

Yeah, a lot *a lot.*
The Universe

Bonus Tips

Here are some extra tips that evolved over the two years I was sharing "Manifesting Change" with live audiences.

Emotion revisited

I wouldn't be surprised if one day I host workshops on the topic of emotions, because they're not only the jewel of all time-space adventures but also our mightiest tool in hastening the manifestations of our thoughts. It's almost impossible to say too much on the subject because the real, underlying reason anybody would want improved health, more friends, or lavish abundance would always be to enhance their own *happiness*. Actually, you could literally look at all of the other things that you might ever want in your life and view them as *cursed hows* toward ultimately experiencing true joy. Therefore, why not just bypass *all* those details and go straight to feeling the joy when visualizing?

And as I mentioned earlier, don't be afraid that by pushing the larger/general happiness button you're not going to get material goodies in your life—that material things *don't matter*. On the contrary, I was advising that you push it because material things *totally rock* and you deserve *all* that you can imagine. And the fastest way to draw them into your life is by focusing on and visualizing joy. Whether visualizing it with or without material details, you unmistakably impress upon the Universe what it is that you really want.

I remember when I met Rhonda Byrne, creator, producer, and visionary of *The Secret*. Before filming started, I asked her not only what *The Secret* was to her, but also what her goal for the film was. Rhonda answered that she wanted to share the secret of the law of attraction and "bring joy to billions." Talk about an ideal end result! Not because it seemed selfless (I see little merit in selfless goals) but because it was *ethereal* from the get-go. Joy to billions.

Many people don't know this, but there was no script for *The Secret*. There wasn't even an insistence on who said what or who spoke when. In fact, there wasn't even an insistence on who was interviewed. Each "teacher" who did end up in front of the camera was given between one to four hours of taping time to just talk about whatever he or she wanted to talk about within the general context of the law of attraction and the power of thought. Talk about latitude!

After gathering about 150 hours of videotape, Rhonda and her expert editorial team followed their intuition and spliced together one speaker after another, whittling it all down to a thread of ninety-two minutes that made flawless sense. If they had insisted on a script, or details, they could have jeopardized not only the production value that was captured but the entire success of Rhonda's end result to bring "joy to billions."

I like this story because it illustrates that you don't have to remember to think of abundance to have abundance, health to have health, or good relationships to have good relationships. If you're thinking happiness, it implies all of that. It implies that everything else in your life is going to be taken care of for you. And this leaves the Universe ample room to shock and delight you in countless ways, day by day and week after week throughout your entire life. You don't have to get specific to experience specifics, thereby leaving infinite room for you to be surprised when your focus is first emotionally defined. The Universe knows exactly what you want, as well as the quickest and easiest way to assemble the details and circumstances that will yield it, and that will invariably include surprises.

A Note from the Universe

The script for the most amazing time in your life is nearing perfection; we're so excited and happy for you ... bravo!
It's complete with friends and laughter, wealth and abundance, health and harmony, and best of all, there are going to be some really neat surprises. Big surprises—really huge, Texas style— and you're going to say, "Bu-bu-but a-a-a- ho-how? Never in all my life have I ever imagined such outrageousness. All my expectations have been exceeded. Never have I even dreamed of being so blessed."

And we're going to say, "Oh yes you did."

And you're going to say, "Oh no I didn't."

And we'll say, "Did."

And you'll say, "Didn't."

And then we'll remind you of those occasions when you simply saw yourself happy: visualizing euphoric happiness, bypassing the details, smiling from ear-to-ear in your mind's eye, pumping your fist, dialing your friend's cell phone number with shaking fingers, happy tears running down your face—when you left all of the hows *to the universe.*

And you're going to say, "Oh."

And we're going to say, through tears of our own, nice hows, *huh?*

Happens all the time,
The Universe

Set up a formal practice for visualizing

Make visualizing a ritual. Come on, this is easy. Easier than yoga, running, or weightlifting, yet it promises so much more. You needn't buy expensive equipment, rent a fancy location, or purchase a whole new wardrobe. Pick a room in your house, pick a chair in that room, pick a time of day, and get a little timer. (If one doesn't come built into your watch or cell phone, then a kitchen egg timer will do just fine.) After five to ten minutes, you're done until tomorrow. You *can* do this; you can treat visualizing with respect. In fact, I bet you already do something like this every day.

I bet you brush your teeth *at least* once a day. I bet you have got a place in your house where you brush your teeth. I bet you've even gone out of your way to buy tools to help you brush your teeth. And the reason you've gone to such great extremes is because you know how profoundly valuable it is. It makes your teeth whiter and keeps them healthy.

Well, if from this day forward you were to do only one of two things for the rest of your life, either brush your teeth or visualize, *visualize*! It can do so much more for you. You can even visualize whiter teeth while you're at it! You religiously brush your teeth even though doing so isn't going to bring you a new relationship, it's not going to increase or decrease the traveling you do, and it's not going to get your entrepreneurial business off the ground. It's not going to bring you into abundance or find you creative fulfilling employment, whereas simply imagining these end results can be the spark that starts bringing them all to you. Just carve out some time every single day (or at least Monday through Friday, as I do) to think those thoughts while visualizing. And happily, these two exercises, brushing your teeth and visualizing, are not mutually exclusive, so I suggest you continue to brush your teeth too!

A Note from the Universe

The trick with imagination . . . is remembering to use it.

Visualize every day.

See you there,
The Universe

Get physical when you're visualizing

Now, I want to advise that this is proprietary information! I don't believe you have ever heard what I'm about to share with you. Mostly because it's a little crazy—or perhaps "unconventional" is a better word.

Knowing how valuable emotion is when visualizing, I realized some time ago that I wasn't actually feeling all that I could feel. Normally, when I would practice my daily four minutes of visualizing, I didn't really *do* anything to feel the emotion, other than perhaps clench my fists, shake, and grimace, as if to say, "Yeah, I'm there, baby. I'm HAPPY!"

But I began to notice that on some days I'd also visualize just briefly, for one minute, right before I began writing the daily Note from the Universe. And when I visualize writing the Note, I don't imagine the process of writing—that's messing with the *cursed hows*. I go beyond to the end result, which for me is that joyful "Whoo-hoo!" feeling that I have when I know I've written really well. That is my end result, *the feeling and emotion*, and it's my only goal every time I sit down to write.

Well, one day, while paying attention to myself doing this mini-visualization, I realized that I wasn't just saying "whoo-hoo" in my mind's eye; no, I was whooping and hollering in my office, pumping my fists in the air, sometimes on my feet, and letting out a big, audible "Yee-haw!" and "Whoo-hoo!" with other animated gestures and sounds. I realized that I was *getting physical*, almost unwittingly, to ramp up the emotion connected to my visualizing and my desired end result. Now why would anyone want to do that? Because emotion—true, raw emotion—is the turbocharger of change for getting fast manifestation results. Emotion brings about what you've been thinking about *faster*, and I couldn't help but notice that this system of mine was working like a charm for my writing.

I decided to add this getting physical step to my daily four-minute visualization. (You may be in a dark and quiet room, but that doesn't mean that you have to sit there like a monk!) Here's a Note from the Universe that actually, though unintentionally at the time of writing, illustrates what you can be doing physically when you're visualizing. I encourage you to "act out" the words in this Note the next time you visualize.

A NOTE FROM THE UNIVERSE

Anyone watching you?

Good! This is a double-secret exercise.

Pretend you just received a phone call with wonderful mind-blowing, life-changing news.

As you put down the receiver, your arms fly up over your head with joy! Pumping your fists and waving your palms like you just crossed a finish line before throngs of adoring fans.

You cover your face with your hands, trying to contain the euphoria . . . but it doesn't work! So you reach for the sky again while shaking your head in disbelief.

You're grinning, crying, and just so happy. Yes!

Life is awesome! And you feel so grateful!

Got it? Good! Now, if someone ever catches you doing this . . . just tell them it was your pet's psychic who called, and they'll forget everything they just saw—especially if you don't have a pet.

You amaze me,
The Universe

These are the antics you can get up to—the theatrics you can play—when you're visualizing. Let it be fun. Be creative. Add a dance step or two, or for that matter, turn up some music, because there are no rules, and it doesn't even have to be a dark and quiet room. *Just feel the joy!*

One of the things I like most about this Note is that it illustrates that you don't even have to have a reason or an imagined set of details or circumstances to feel the joy when you visualize: just feel the joy! In the Note, it didn't say that you've just won the lottery or that someone you find very attractive is interested in you; you can leave all of those details to universal principles. It'll still do its job of bringing that joy back to you like a boomerang on this plane of manifestation that we live on. The Universe will literally rush around behind the curtains of time and space to rearrange circumstances so that you will have the actual physical and material reasons to finally manifest that joy you put out there when you were visualizing. Of course, you can and you *must* take action in the general direction of your dreams, but we haven't quite gotten to that part of the book just yet. In the meantime, visualizing is the least you can do to get the most.

Now *that's* playing the Matrix!

5

The Power to Have It All

The power to have it all arises from the actions we take toward our end results—actions that will predispose us to life's magic. But based on what I've already shared, the actions you have to take are very simple—baby steps, really. You don't even have to move in the correct direction as long as you're doing your best to move in the direction that seems correct (or as close to correct as you can, however uncertain you may feel). Even moving in the "wrong" direction at least puts you within reach of guidance; and then through serendipities, new friends, and observations, you'll be gently coaxed into making a *legal* U-turn.

So in this chapter, rather than calling upon you to take action to harness "the power to have it all," I'm going to throw a curve ball by suggesting that it's *the perspectives you hold on your life and dreams that will automatically influence the actions you take*. This means that the key to putting yourself into full-power mode, throwing yourself into the direction of your dreams (step two in the mechanics of manifestation), comes from getting a handle on or changing your present outlook and worldview, which is comparatively far easier than the old-fashioned ways of forcing yourself to work harder and wiser.

Taking action, most typically, is automatic. We don't have to think about everything we do before we do it; we actually go through most of our daily lives guided by habit and routine. Yet by establishing a new point of view that's in alignment with our end results, one that implies "we've arrived" rather than implying "wouldn't it be nice," our day-to-day actions automatically begin to change, literally predisposing us to life's magic—the so-called accidents and coincidences.

A Note from the Universe

Be there. Go there now and never leave. Imagine that your dreams have already come true. Live your life from that mind-set. Predicate your behavior on that reality, not the illusions that now surround you. Filter every thought, question, and answer from there. Let your focus shift and be born again—because dwelling from, not upon, the space you wish to inherit is the fastest way to change absolutely everything.

See the difference?
The Universe

The Mansion of Your Wildest Dreams

There is a vast difference between dwelling *from* and dwelling *upon* the life you wish to lead. It's the difference between acting *as if* you're already *at* your end result, living your life from that viewpoint (to the degree that you can), rather than gazing upon it wistfully from afar with a perspective of "have not." It closes the gap and presumes success: you've *already* arrived.

Dwelling *from* is your ticket. Dwelling *from* can be likened to (and you can do this *today*) creating in your mind's eye the "mansion" of your wildest dreams—a mansion that's not just your home but a symbol for the full-blown life of your dreams. From this day forward, metaphorically, you are to gaze *through* its windows *at* the world outside, letting *this* view shape your behavior with regard to anything and everyone. Live your life from *that* outlook, the mind-set that says, "I *have* arrived; I *live* in abundance; I *have* new-found health and beauty, more friends, more laughter, and harmonious relationships." That's moving *into* your mansion, instead of remaining on the outside looking in.

This is entirely about perspective—and we get to choose it! If you can make this leap, "pretending" in a manner of speaking, and move into this mansion with your thoughts and your behavior, the actions you take will automatically shift into alignment with your end results. And life's magic will take it from there.

Case Studies

Shifting to new perspectives is something that we often do naturally. I look at my own life and see proof of this everywhere, and most typically I've shifted perspectives without even realizing it. But of course, once you realize you've done it unconsciously, you can start doing it deliberately.

I can remember when I was in college, just a few months away from graduating, and my roommate and I started speculating about what it would be like living in the "real world" as adults. As you can imagine, at twenty-two years old this seemed like foreign territory. One of the concepts that we were trying to grasp was the idea of earning an annual salary. I mean, we sure loved the sound of that word—*salary*—but what did it really mean?

I wanted to be hired by one of the big eight accounting firms of the time. And I knew that while there was a range of salaries they were paying, the median was about $18,500 per year. Yeah, I was about to become independently wealthy! Still, that annual number of $18,500 kind of left me cold. I couldn't really get my head around it and neither could my roommate, so we pulled out our calculators and started crunching numbers. It turned out that $18,500 a year is more than $1,500 a month. Eureka! This shook us to our core; now we could taste it, we could grasp it. We figured that our rent would be $150 to $200 a month and a car payment, if I went crazy (which I did), would be around $200 to $250 a month, leaving us with about $700 a month, every month (after expenses and taxes), for *beer*! Whoo-hoo!

Getting the Car of My Dreams

We could now begin seeing what our new lives were going to look and *feel* like. But this wasn't where I stopped. It's never enough to just have the thought; *you must take action*. I was ready to start *basing my behavior* on this new view of reality. So I called up my parents and said, "Good news, I'm about to become independently wealthy, but ... um ... Dad, I could use your help. Would you mind co-signing the loan for my new car 'cause I have no credit?"

He was happy to oblige, and just for yuks we went to a dealership the next weekend I was home to assess the possibilities. My dream car at the time was a Fiat Spider. Oh my gosh, what a beautiful car! Except we discovered that this was the last year—1983—that Fiat was exporting to the United States, which meant that whatever was on the car lot was all they had. And in St. Petersburg, Florida, they only had four Fiat Spiders left, all of them dark green. We were told the red ones went to California a long time ago, where they had quickly sold out.

Well, that didn't discourage me; I was young and naïve! I took a brochure, which included a full-page photo of a *red* Spider, and taped it on the wall next to my dormitory's bedroom door. For the next two months, every time I left my dorm room, I checked out the car of my dreams: red with a gold pinstripe, low profile, alloy wheels, convertible, wood paneling on the dashboard—wow! Well, fast-forward and you can probably guess what happened. On graduation day, Dad drove to my commencement ceremony in my new Fiat, which he had co-signed for on my behalf. It was a *red* Fiat Spider with every detail included in the photo that I stared at multiple times every day for two months. To this day, I don't know where he found a red one, but this car story is just a footnote to the bigger story of landing my first job.

Hard Knocks

Now I had my dream car, but then the sand started shifting beneath my feet because I didn't have a job! According to *TIME Magazine*, it was the leanest hiring time for college graduates since World War II. Great. Day after day, week after week, and month after painful month, I was pounding the pavement looking for work, knowing that I had to support my red Fiat Spider. The situation became so desperate that within two months after graduating, my savings were only enough for one, possibly two more car payments—and that was it. The consequences of running out of savings were unthinkable. Fortuitously, if you will, or perhaps out of sympathy, my father's accountant gave me a call and said, "Mike, I hear you're looking for a job. Come on down for an interview."

The interview went really well, and a letter followed in the mail that said, "Dear Mr. Dooley, we're pleased to extend an invitation for you to join our firm at an annual salary of $12,500." This was a major poke in the eye! I remember looking at that letter thinking, "That's *not* me; that's not who I am. It's never going to happen; I have a *reputation* to maintain," even though I lived at home with my mom at the time. I told the company, no; there was just no way. It didn't add up and wasn't how I saw my path in life unfolding. Panic time!

I scrambled, writing résumés for every industry and profession I could think of that would take an accounting background (banking, insurance, brokerage), and pounded the pavement for another thirty days. That's when I learned through a neighbor that PricewaterhouseCoopers, the Tiffany's of the Big Eight accounting firms, was unexpectedly hiring out of season because they had just landed a huge hospital as a new client.

Just As I Pictured It

I got the interview and the letter came a week later: "Dear Mr. Dooley, we're pleased to extend you an offer to join our firm at an annual salary of $18,500." Bingo! Reading the letter I was stunned to recall that this was the *exact amount* my roommate and I had picked to pieces and determined to be an ideal salary just six months earlier. Very quickly, the light went on, and it dawned on me that *I had set a bar*! Moreover, not only had I created an end result—though that's not the terminology I used back then—*I had been basing my behavior on that vision (perspective)*: buying the car and turning down a job for far less money.

For about three weeks I was walking in the clouds, feeling like the king of the world because of what *I* had manifested. And then it suddenly dawned on me: "Hmmm, why hadn't I raised the bar a lot higher?"

Raising the Bar

Where are your bars? Here's a hint: they're revealed by everything you think, say, and do. They're a function of your present perspectives that give rise to your expectations—expectations that concern how much you can earn, how much you'll allow yourself to weigh, and what kind of behavior from others you will, or will not, tolerate. You may put up with X, and under certain circumstances you could put up with Y, but under *no* circumstances will you ever put up with Z. These are your bars. And guess what? They're arbitrary. You've arbitrarily set them. You could have demanded more or settled for less, and this is especially exciting because it means you can arbitrarily move them any time, putting them in places where they may serve you even more than where they had been before.

If you're not sure of where your bars are, begin paying attention to your conversations; start noticing what your behavior is. And if you're not pleased with what you're preparing for, change your perspective.

A friend from England revealed one of her bars when we were discussing international travel. We were talking about

Thailand when her eyes suddenly opened as wide as saucers. She said, "Oh! I've heard that Thailand has the best youth hostels!" And then just as suddenly, she realized that even though she currently had no plans to visit Thailand, if and when she does go, she mentally sees herself staying in a youth hostel.

Now, there's nothing wrong with staying at youth hostels; if hostels work for you, as they obviously do for my friend, then no problem. Stay wherever you want—sleep under the stars. If, however, you dream of visiting Thailand too, and you'd prefer to stay at a luxury hotel, then it's time to stop imagining yourself staying at a youth hostel. My message here is not about the "bling"; it's about understanding that your present perspectives are what set the bars in your life—that you reveal these perspectives in your thoughts, words, and behavior, and when you don't like a bar's setting, you can raise or lower it.

For example, right now, imagine yourself sitting on a plane, flying to some exotic international destination, such as Hong Kong, New Delhi, or Sydney. Long journey, huh? Imagine it. I bet you see more than one movie during all of your connecting flights. And I sure hope you can sleep on a plane! Actually, can you sleep when you fly? OK. Point made.

Pop quiz: In this imaginary flight, did you see yourself seated in coach, business, or first class? Instinctively and automatically, based upon our life perspective, our imagination takes us to "places" that are in alignment with our worldview at the time.

Want to change your experience? Pay attention to where your bars are. Remember, these are just thoughts that we're talking about, and you can change those! Why not see yourself in first class or at a five-star hotel *if* those things would please you? And they're more than just thoughts; they're the building blocks of your tomorrows. All it takes is your permission to think new ones. And then regularly—daily, weekly or monthly, depending on what the dream is—base your behavior in some small way on those new settings: pretend you're flying first class or, every now and then, if you fly a lot, splurge on first class seats, even if only for the short flights.

If you can give yourself that little shift, big wheels start turning behind the curtains of time and space that will rearrange your life and start bringing you new customers, friends, or insights—whatever it is that you need—until the time arrives when it is no longer a game of make-believe. It's your life.

Let's Go to Ferrari!

My taste in cars changed significantly after a few years of having my Fiat Spider. Not that I wasn't always in love with it, but I started to acquire a taste for more expensive cars. And without even noticing it, I became obsessed with BMWs. I could tell you anything and everything about them during that phase of my life, and it just so happened that while under their spell, I visited a friend in Miami one weekend. On the first morning, I woke to the sound of his sons running through the house, yelling, "Daddy! Daddy! Daddy! Let's go to Ferrari! Let's go to Ferrari!" His boys were only four and seven years old, so I couldn't help but wonder if I had woken up in some weird dream. It turned out that their dad occasionally treated them with a trip to the local Ferrari dealership as a reward for good behavior. Jeez, when I was a kid and had earned "points" after *months* of being good, my parents would take me to feed the ducks at a local park!

Anyway, I joined my friend and his kids at Ferrari that morning, and lo and behold, he and his sons knew every Ferrari on the floor. Moreover, all the sales people knew my friend and his sons. And it turned out, my friend knew Ferraris like I knew BMWs, and I was indignant! The audacity. I remember thinking, what gave him the right? Where does he get off thinking so big? Of course, I wasn't really scandalized by his high expectations but more by my own comparatively low ones. Well, the rest of story is predictable. You can probably guess what kind of car I ended up driving and still drive to this day—BMW. And you can guess what kind of car my friend ended up driving and still drives to this day—Ferrari. We arbitrarily set our bars, and perhaps by me sharing this, you're beginning to sense some of yours.

When it came to first writing this material a couple of years ago, I vividly remembered that experience and my sense of indignation, because it was just so impressive to me that somebody my age (at the time) could have the nerve (and the courage) to focus upon and think about owning a Ferrari and then *move in that direction*! It was eye-opening, to say the least. But this memory taunted me during my writing because then, and to this day, I could do the Ferrari, yet I haven't. I hear that all-too-familiar inner voice, "Mike, you don't *need* a Ferrari! Look at all that's going on in your life: all the travel, investments, and adventure!" And then another voice reminds me, "Mike, *nobody* needs a Ferrari. That's not why you get a Ferrari." Then I counter that I really don't care that much about having one, and the debate continues. So I've still got a tug-of-war going on somewhat. But, I'm an adventurer like you, and the learning and discovery process never ends.

The important thing is to recognize that you've got bars, and they're plainly visible once you know about them. And once you find out where yours are, you can change them—change not only your point of view but also nudge yourself along, as you'll soon see, with token behavioral changes, so that your actions mirror and reconfirm the view from the mansion of your wildest dreams.

He Really Did Rock Us

One last story on perspectives and how they shape our behavior and the actions we take: I saw a "rockumentary" on MTV a few years ago about the British rock band Queen, arguably one of the biggest rock bands of the twentieth century. Since their lead singer, Freddie Mercury, had passed away many years before this documentary was made, they could only create it by interviewing his surviving band mates. Interestingly, every one of them said that Freddie Mercury was the biggest rock star they had ever met in their entire lives—from the day they first met him he was larger than life.

Yet on the day that they each met Freddie Mercury for the first time, he had no hits to his name. He was flat broke—so poor that he slept on the floors of his band mates' homes in successive turns so that he wouldn't burn out his welcome. Still, they all agreed he was *already* the biggest rock star they had ever met, because in Freddie's mind he was already there. That's where he set the bar and *that's what he predicated his behavior upon*, to the degree that he could. They each said that all he could think about, talk about, eat, sleep, and breathe were the stadiums they would one day fill to the brim; the theatrics that would make them famous; the

costumes that would dazzle the crowds; and the perform-
ances that would rock the world. He was already dwelling
from the place of being a legend.

And when you imagine *your* end result and start moving
with it, no matter what it is, whether superstardom or just
plain happiness, *it has to happen.* The right people, inspiration,
and circumstances will land on your path; it's the absolute
law. It's how *thoughts become things.* And it all begins with a
new outlook, which, once adopted, automatically throws you
into motion.

Here's a Note that should test your perspectives!

A NOTE FROM THE UNIVERSE

*Okay! The reservation's been made and a private Beechcraft
400A jet will be yours, with experienced staff, advanced
multimedia hookups for each passenger, and faux leopard-skin
sleeper recliners throughout, for any twenty-one days that
you choose, just as soon as you arrange payment of
the $368,750—in advance.*

Fuel of course will cost extra. A lot extra.

*Now, repeat after me: "You have to be joking! Faux leopard skin
is so early 2000. What else do they have?!"*

*Cool! Now stay with this perspective, because this kind of
transaction takes place every single day. And because perspectives
summon circumstances that change fortunes.*

*See you in Cannes,
The Universe*

Guidelines for Raising the Bar

Raising the bar, or lowering it, depending on what we're talking about, is easy. Here are some very simple guidelines that will help show you the way.

Don't Condition Your Behavior On the Illusions

The following sentence is perhaps the most important sentence I will share with you in this entire book: *Learn not to condition your behavior on the illusions of time, space, and matter.* Though, perhaps I should add to that sentence "at least not exclusively," as living in time and space clearly requires recognition of "what is." Conditioning or predicating your behavior *exclusively*, or even significantly, on the physical world around you simply perpetuates the conditions you're living in. With such a paradox, the solution is to simply "play both ends toward the middle," which essentially means dealing with the physical world to the extent that you must, while at the same time dealing with *and physically preparing for* the world of your dreams. Keep your day job, but physically prepare for and act as if the life of your dreams was also at hand.

I concede that keeping your day job could be viewed by some as a cop-out or half measure, yet far worse would be "testing" the system, or your faith, to the degree of risking the very roof over your head, your health, or your friendships. Such an extreme simply isn't necessary as long as you're consistently aware of your end results and are consistently doing what you can, from where you are and with what you've got, to move in their direction. Sure, you could be like Freddie Mercury—quit your job, and sleep on your friend's floor with an attitude of "never surrender"—but maybe consider too that Mariah Carey was once a waitress, Elvis Presley a machinist, and J. K. Rowling a full-time mom while they all *simultaneously* pursued careers that would eventually make them household names on every continent.

Losing weight

Since perspective is such an important concept, let's look at the example of wanting to lose weight. If your only action were to buy diet, low-fat, low-calorie, low-this and low-that foods, such behavior would perpetuate your condition (no matter how much visualizing you did) because every single purchase would be like screaming to the Universe, "I have a weight problem!" And the Universe would reply, "I heard you the first seven hundred times, and it is done!"

By believing in your issue to such a degree that you're predicating *all* your behavior on it, you will be unwittingly and magically predisposed to all the wrong foods at all the wrong times. Your metabolism will slow down, your energy will diminish, your enthusiasm will evaporate, and everything will seem to work against you as universal principles conspire to bring your behavioral end results to fruition. The Universe will be confirming what you would have been putting out there, which is that you *can't* lose weight and that you *do* have a weight problem.

Instead, start changing your behavior *incrementally* so that at least some of the time it's conditioned on the dream. Play both ends to the middle. Behave conventionally by watching what you eat and choosing wisely, conservatively, and carefully; but also splurge with behavior that reinforces the notion that you have already achieved success. Allow yourself the occasional indulgence as if you were already your ideal weight; *be* the person of your dreams, if only playfully acting. Just be careful, as this goes both ways.

For example, if you love chocolate cake and occasionally go out for a meal at a nice restaurant that has chocolate cake on the dessert menu, I don't care how much you weigh, have a dang piece of cake! Give it to yourself. Act the part. Enjoy it the way you would if you already had the body you've always dreamed you'd have. Don't, however, eat the entire cake. This is not what the "dreamed-of you" would do. Again, it works both ways. Act the part—the *whole* part—and enjoy your life and the rewards of your envisioned success today.

By occasionally acting outside of the norm, you'll literally install new beliefs as your behavior alerts the Universe, life's magic, and your inner witness that things are changing. And if you repeatedly change your behavior, such as how you window shop for the skinnier, slimmer you, while also watching what you eat and choosing words that serve you, *look out world!*

Summoning abundance

If you've got money, and you're hoarding it all for a rainy day; or if you're looking at the stock market and what the world economy is doing, and you're basing all of your behavior on these "illusions," this does not speak well of your belief in the inevitable arrival of great avalanches of abundance rushing toward you, now does it? Splurge here and there, assuming you've got enough money for small indulgences. BUT, to repeat a bit of advice from *Infinite Possibilities*, *never* spend money you don't have (with credit cards, for example) if you can't readily pay it off. It simply isn't necessary, as the number of things you can do to demonstrate faith is infinite and most require no expenditures whatsoever.

I caught myself basing my behavior solely on physical circumstances while I was booking a flight to Atlanta, Georgia, on my first world tour seven years ago. During the tour, I had flown virtually everywhere first class (the first time I had ever done so in my life). My speaking date in Atlanta was coming up, and two weeks before, I found out there were only six people signed up to attend this five-hour program. I lamented, "Dang, six people. It's hardly worth going." But, of course, I wasn't going to back out.

When I started to price flights, I found it would cost $1,200 to fly first class from Orlando to Atlanta and back. This is only a forty-five minute flight each way, and by comparison, would only cost $200 to fly coach. So I got caught up in the illusion trap. I was assessing the illusions around me without even realizing it, thinking to myself, "Look, six people are signed up now. Maybe by start time there will be twelve or fifteen. If I spend $1,200 bucks on this short flight, it's going to be a red-letter day: not a pretty financial picture. I don't *need* to fly first class."

And then the light went on in my head. "Mike, you are a highly sought-after, world-class professional speaker (my dream and intended end result)," I said to myself. "And Mike, such folks don't fly coach, no matter *who* is on the other end of the flight. Flying coach as a wanna-be professional speaker will not serve you in becoming the real deal."

Then the coin dropped even farther. This was not just about me being tough with myself; this was not about saying, "Oh dang it, I've got to walk the walk. You know I'm going to have to splurge on a first class ticket." So I changed the self-talk to sound more like, "Whoa! First class! Enjoy it! And real-ize, Mike, by making this demonstration, in spite of the illusions that now surround you, you are going to be *forcing* life's magic, the Universe, to create circumstances where you *are* that highly sought-after, world-class professional speaker. Not only will you be given or infused with great content to share with your audiences, but your audiences will grow as your end result is made manifest!" Don't use only logic and your physical senses to make all of your decisions.

To clarify, I *did* have the money in this situation. I'm not saying *you* should spend money you don't have. But by pur-chasing that ticket and moving with my dreams, my first world tour's average audience size ended up being seventy people. My second world tour, which has now concluded, averaged 170 people. (Incidentally, the attendance in Atlanta ended up being thirty-five people.) This kind of playful act-ing—conditioning your behavior on your dream and not just basing it on the illusions—is pure power, even if sporadic or piecemeal (or only when you can afford it).

Increasing trust in a relationship

Maybe you're in a relationship where your partner hasn't always been totally honest or forthright with you. You could start guarding your heart and physically preparing for more of the same, but for the metaphysical reasons I've already shared, that will likely perpetuate their behavior. On the other hand, if you *really* want your partner to step up to the plate; if you want to raise the bar and maximize the *probability* that his or her behavior is going to improve, then you need to start acting with confidence in them—acting as though you trust your partner and that they are trustworthy. Yup, you need to put your heart out there because *nothing else* will ensure a greater *likelihood* of improved behavior than you preparing to receive it. Raise the bar! He or she will see it and will intellectually or subliminally know what's going on. You're going to be inviting him or her to improve when you stop preparing for the worst. Bottom line: it's their life and they're going to do what they want; their thoughts will become their things. But if you want to maximize your chances of seeing an improvement, prepare for it. Physically prepare for it.

Having a job you hate

All too often, and understandably, people in a job they dislike have the attitude that once they're in the job of their dreams—once they finally find that special place that they're supposed to be—*then* they're going to shine. Uh-Uh, it doesn't work that way. Start shining *today*. Start living your life as if you were onstage and a million eyes were watching because, in a sense, they are. *Life* is watching. *You* are watching. Bad behavior does not beget good behavior and neither does it summon the dream job.

When I started writing the daily Notes from the Universe, those first emails I sent only went out to thirty-six people. But even then, I always wrote to the absolute best of my ability, as if I had a million subscribers. And today, I'm more than a third of the way there.

I gave my first "Thoughts Become Things" speech to fourteen people in my Toastmasters Club, but I wrote it for the world, and now, ten years later, it's still good enough that I've incorporated parts of it into live presentations on five continents. Not that you have to smack the ball out of the park and blow everyone's mind every single minute of every single day; I certainly didn't, not as a writer or a speaker. But I did my best with what I had and from where I was, and so can you.

To summarize and repeat again because this point is so important, *learn not to condition your behavior on the illusions.* Instead, condition your behavior on your dream—the view from the end result of your wildest dreams.

Keep Busy, Don't Stop

As long as you want change, *keep* busy. *Stay* active. The more you do, the more opportunities life's magic will have to reach you. Never does the day dawn that you're "done." Nor, I should add, would you ever want it to dawn, as long as you're moving to the beat of your own drummer (which I'll talk about in the next chapter, "Opening the Floodgates").

I remember just a few years ago, before my life as a writer and speaker really blasted off, I was catching up with a friend I had met five years earlier at Toastmasters. In our conversation, I mentioned something about the chapter we had once been members of (he had long since stopped attending meetings). "You're still a member of Toastmasters???" he said incredulously. He was shocked to discover that I was still an active member, especially since he knew I was already speaking professionally around the world.

Sheepishly, I admitted I was and then explained my rationale that until I was too busy to attend, whether because of work or my social life, it was a resource that could still make me a better speaker while providing me with social and business networking opportunities at the same time. I could have so easily shrugged off my membership and the work it entailed, thinking I was good enough or that the Universe was handling my career, but to this day I know better. The more we put ourselves out there and accept the responsibility for our happiness, fulfillment, and personal growth, we exponentially increase the opportunities the Universe has to arrange things on our behalf and propel us forward *faster*.

Incidentally, I'm quite pleased to report that within a year or so of that meeting with my friend, and ever since, I *have been* almost unimaginably busy and unable to attend any Toastmaster meetings, now possessing a wildly fuller life in every regard—*thanks in part to my seven years as a member*. The point I'm emphasizing here is that even after we garner a lot of career (or whatever) momentum, if we still want more change, it behooves us to continually play both ends to the middle, conventionally practicing, preparing, and networking (as in my example), while simultaneously dreaming and acting with faith that the ship of our dreams has already arrived. Dance with your dreams, not just with the illusions that now surround you.

Don't Sweat the Direction You First Move In

I repeatedly meet people who are so unsure of the steps they should take that they take none. They're waiting on the sidelines, some with a job that they hate and some with no job at all, as if Larry King is suddenly going to call for an interview and change their lives forever. *He's not calling*. Take action! Remember the digital satellite navigation system analogy: taking action, even in the wrong direction, is better than leaving your car in park. So don't sweat it. Get going.

A Note from the Universe

*Rarely are the first steps in a journey anything like the final ones,
either in direction, pace, or grace. So please believe me when I
tell you that none of those things are even half as important
as the fact that there are steps at all.*

*By the time you're really rolling, it will be in a
direction you cannot even imagine now.*

So please, for the time being, just roll.

Tallyho,
The Universe

Understand that Everything Matters

You're always on the stage, 24/7, whether you're with a group
of friends or all alone. You're constantly demonstrating and
revealing to the Universe (*and* yourself) where your bars are
and what you expect to happen next in your life. So if you're
talking to yourself in the mirror unfavorably, not good. If
you're talking to your best friend in the middle of the night
about how guys always do this or how girls always do that, not
good. Watch yourself. Listen. Pay attention. With great power
comes great responsibility, and it's important to know that
when it comes to your outlook; you need to take responsibility
for it all. Everything matters.

The upside to this is that we have endless opportunities to
demonstrate and reveal what our new perspectives are by a little
playful acting or acting with faith. The Universe once said in a
Note, "Thinking big but acting small is the same as thinking

small." And although you're no doubt nodding your head in agreement as you read these words right now, if you're not actually predicating more and more of your behavior on your dreams in the days to come, it's the same as not agreeing at all.

Use Your Head *and* Your Heart

This advice is particularly geared toward people who are new to metaphysical thinking. There's a tendency for such folks, at first, to live exclusively from the heart, completely discounting and disregarding any of their thoughts that seem remotely logical. And it's from these people that I hear some pretty interesting ideas. For example, kitten legwarmers! "Oh yeah, they're going to be *huge* in 2011, Mike. I know that my *thoughts become things*. I know all things are possible. Abundance is my birthright. Kitten legwarmers are going to be the rage!"

Kitten legwarmers will *never* be the rage. Kittens will never need legwarmers, and I challenge anybody to have an *intellectual* conviction that kitten legwarmers will ever be viable. It's just that people are so afraid to let go of one idea, fearing they might not have another one. ("But heck, who needs another idea with an invention like kitten legwarmers when the Universe is riding shotgun?") And so, they attach to a *cursed how* that's supposed to bring them fame and fortune while making kittens and their owners the world over an even happier lot. They're attaching themselves and their future successes to their heart-heavy ideas just like others attach to a property they're trying to list, or to a stock that they want to go up, or to a book they just wrote, or to a specific person as a partner, not realizing they're limiting the Universe from reaching them with something, or someone, even better.

All of this could be avoided by getting a little logical. Now, logic *is* generally overrated in our society, and I'm not saying to use it because intelligence is all that valuable; it's not. But when you use a little logic, you can sometimes chart a path of least resistance between your otherwise invisible limiting beliefs. If it feels right intellectually *and* in your heart, at least as close as you can get to feeling peace in both places, then chances are you're not going to be contending with otherwise challenging beliefs that might say, "That's impractical, that's unrealistic, or don't go there." Use your head and your heart when choosing the path to go down.

Pretending Counts—Big Time

Cher used to practice signing her autograph in front of the mirror before she was ever famous. Larry King used to interview his childhood friends in his parents' basement, holding a hammer as a make-believe microphone. Jim Carrey was living homeless out of his car in Hollywood, California, when one day, broke but still dreaming, he had the inspiration to write himself a check for twenty million dollars. Today, other folks *do* write checks to Jim Carrey for twenty million dollars. Pretending counts, big time.

I shared a story along these lines in my last audio program, "Leveraging the Universe and Engaging the Magic," and it now has an addendum to it: When I was in Brisbane, Australia, during my first world tour, I met a cool lady at the VIP dinner I hosted after my daylong talk. She was telling those of us at the table that in addition to visualizing a new man in her life, she decided to start *pretending* that he was already there.

She cleaned out the clutter in her two-car garage, stopped parking in the middle of it, and started parking on "her side," pretending that she needed to make room for his car and acting as if he was already in her life. She said she went to one of her two master bedroom closets and cleaned it out from top to bottom, making room for his stuff even though there was no one in her life yet. She stopped sleeping in the middle of the king size bed and started sleeping on "her side," pretending he was there. And of course, the happy news shared during the dinner was that her date that evening was "proof" that this pretending worked, as they were now happily living together in her home.

Fast-forward two years to when I received a phone call from Rhonda Byrne. *The Secret* had already become a blockbuster DVD, and now she was writing the book edition. "Mike, the story you told in your audio program about the lady in Brisbane has always stayed with me. May I use it?" I told her I'd have to check and see.

Sure enough, the approval came, along with a PS: "By the way, we're married!" Pretending counts big time: it's huge!

A Note from the Universe

Here's what I ask folks who aspire to being fabulously rich:

"Couldn't you just pretend you're a multimillionaire?"

"You know, right after you're done pretending you're not?"

See you in the teller line,
The Universe

It's all pretend. Your life, right now, is just pretend. We live in the illusionary jungles of time, space, and matter. And the way you manifest change is to start physically pretending, as if your life has already changed.

Doing Your Best Is Always Enough

People from my audiences often approach me to ask, "Mike, how do you visualize? I don't know if I'm doing it right." Or, "Mike, when I pretend or act *as if,* I feel like I'm lying. How do you do this?" Plus lots of other how-to questions. And the answer is invariably the same: there's no *one* way. Try several things. Just do your best; it will always be enough.

There was once a Note from the Universe that essentially said, *If you're visualizing, you're doing it right. If you're acting with faith, you're doing it right. If you're choosing your words wisely, you're doing it right.* And that's all you need to know. Don't think that there's some advanced insight or technique involved that you just aren't privy to yet. If you just give whatever it is your best shot, it will *always* be enough. My entire life has shown me this.

I also get questions like, "Mike, I'm worried about my baggage; you know, all the programming I received since the day I was born. I don't know what I believe or don't believe anymore." Or "What about our subconscious thoughts? How do we know what they are?" Or "Mike, how do I stay positive? Sometimes I can't control my negative, fearful thoughts." In all cases, I say, "Don't worry about it!" And again, "Just do your best; it'll always be enough." As I've laid out at length in *Infinite Possibilities,* it's *as if* our positive thoughts are 10,000 times more powerful than our negative thoughts.

To recap, a thought is a thought is a thought. They all strive to become things, and it's only one person's judgment that says a thought is positive or negative, but we've already established in the first chapter that we are not here accidentally. You existed before this life in time and space began, and you meticulously chose the stage you were born upon *so that you could thrive*. With a little deductive reasoning and simple life observation, this becomes blatantly obvious. We're all innately driven to better ourselves—to strive, to learn, and to grow—and in spite of these primitive times during which most have failed to see themselves as the natural-born creators they are, we still find success *more* than we do failure!

Nobody comes here to be poor their entire life. Nobody comes here to be sick their entire life. Nobody comes here to be lonely their entire life. If the conditions of your life so far have been displeasing, you can change them; that's what this book is all about. Life is about adventure, adventure is about challenge, and in the vast majority of cases, challenges are chosen to be overcome. It would be more apt to note that if you were born into poverty, you chose that life to live in abundance! Poverty *wasn't* meant to be your mainstay. And while you can readily find seeming exceptions to these claims by pointing to starving children in Africa, or even here in the United States, these are nevertheless the exceptions. *Rare* exceptions with relatively easy-to-understand, big-picture explanations, as will be touched on in chapter 7, "Understanding Adversity." This book, however, is for the hundreds of millions of Americans and the billions of other nationals alive today all over the world, who can readily and easily begin affecting deliberate and exciting change in their lives once they learn the truth about who we are, why we're here, and what we are each capable of doing.

Because of your original, persistent, and innate intent to thrive on a stage you chose for that purpose, when you think a positive thought, it immediately goes with the grain and the energies that match your reason for being. It's already in alignment with who you really are and what you're really about. It makes sense, and it adds to the fire of all your desires. Whereas, when you think a negative thought, no matter how dark your life has seemed so far, it doesn't fit. It *doesn't* make sense. You're not here to be unhappy, sick, lonely, or broke. If you think a negative thought, it contradicts the magnificence of your being.

Therefore, while a thought is a thought is a thought, it's *as if* your positive thoughts are 10,000 times more powerful than your negative thoughts, and, if anything, that number is a gross understatement. Accordingly, if you just do your best, not giving undo energy and attention to your so-called baggage or subconscious thoughts, it will always be enough. Don't worry about your doubts and insecurities. Press on. Vincent van Gogh once said, "If you hear a voice within you say 'you cannot paint,' then by all means paint, and that voice will be silenced."

Understand Why You Do What You Do

The above heading is so important because it's what enables you to enjoy the journey. You are not the home-run hitter. Your action part—the baby steps—is not supposed to be hitting the home-run that saves or makes your life. That's way too much pressure, and that's not why you do what you do. Instead, understand that the real reason for your actions is to give the Universe an opportunity to reach its hand into your daily affairs with its seeming miracles and magic. Your part, physically speaking, involves little more than showing up!

If you're out there in the world, constantly knocking on new doors and turning over new stones, then you're reachable, and that's a whole lot easier than having to go out all alone and be a hero. It would never work. Instead, you need to see yourself as the pitcher, pitching the ball to the Universe by the various actions you take so that the Universe can hit the home-run. Which it can and *will* do as long as you keep pitching—even when your actions may seem paltry and feeble, especially compared to your grandiose dreams, and even when it seems you've already pitched a lot of foul balls.

This brings me to another question that arises frequently from audience members: "Mike, if I'm *not* supposed to mess with the *cursed hows* but *I am* supposed to physically move in the general direction of my dreams, isn't this a contradiction?" Again, what makes a *cursed how* a *cursed how* is not *what* you're doing but *how you view* what you're doing. If you view yourself as the home-run hitter, it's a *cursed how*. If you view yourself as the pitcher, with each pitch representing action you take that can get the Universe in on the game, then it's not a *cursed how*; it's you moving in the general direction of your dreams.

Imagine, for instance, two people who each join the same Rotary club. One of them might be viewing it as a chance to meet "Mr. Big." Yeah, they're going to meet Mr. Big, they're going to sit with him at lunch and tell him funny jokes, and he's going to *love* them. And then Mr. Big is going to list his house with this person. That's messing with the *cursed hows*.

Another person can join the very same Rotary club, but as they view it, they're just knocking on one of many doors. They may also join other service clubs, make cold calls at work, or network in other ways. This person doesn't know which door will provide results but isn't worried because there are a lot of irons in the proverbial fire. Their attendance at Rotary can then be enjoyed. They may sit next to Mr. Big or maybe meet an even bigger fish. Maybe it'll be *Mrs.* Big! Or maybe their membership won't add to their business connections but will be seized by life's magic to improve their social life, while the Universe uses their other pitches to reach them on the business front. From this perspective, none of this person's actions will be *cursed hows.*

To differentiate it one more time, what makes something a *cursed how* is not *what* you do, but *how you view* what you do. When you finally understand why you're taking such actions—because you have an infallible Universe there to connect the dots of your actions—you can then move around freely, finally enjoying the journey without carrying the weight of the world on your shoulders.

A Note from the Universe

Invariably, when big dreams come true, and I mean BIG, *there is a total metamorphosis of one's life. Thoughts change, words change, decisions are made differently. Gratitude is tossed about like rice at a wedding. Priorities are rearranged and optimism soars. Yeah, those folks can be really annoying.*

You could have guessed all of that, huh? But would you have guessed that these changes invariably come about before, not after, the big dream's manifestation.

Invariably means always, The Universe

You can do this! You can change your thoughts, reshape your words, and make decisions differently. You can toss about gratitude like rice at a wedding. You can rearrange your priorities and alter your viewpoint. That's practically all it takes. New actions will follow automatically, yet you can hasten the entire process profoundly by beginning to predicate as much of your behavior as possible on the life of your dreams instead of solely upon the circumstances that now surround you.

You Can Do This!

I'd like to wrap up this chapter with an exercise called "Acting Lessons." Acting, or pretending, is something my mother, my brother, and I do on a regular basis when we get together, and we've been doing it for years. As I said earlier, about once a month we get together to share new readings, talk about new epiphanies or insights, walk through guided visualizations, or whatever comes to mind.

Playing Make-Believe

At one of our meetings, many, many years ago, we started pretending in our discussion that some of our biggest dreams had already come true. It's a bit out there but always fun. I would say something like, "Mom, I've just finished building my new home on the windward side of Oahu; you're going to love it! And, hey, when you're finished filming the animated version of *Dandelion* with Steven Spielberg in L.A., why don't you take a week off, jump on a plane, and visit? Andy, you can do the same. When you're finished painting the town red in Paris, come on over with Mom! I'll even let you borrow my jet."

Then Andy one-upped me, saying, "Thanks, but I'll take a rain check. I'm planning to spend that week at the Riviera with Jennifer Aniston. Besides, your jet is just too small for my entourage." We'd go all the way around, playing that not only our *own* wildest dreams had already come true but so had each others. It's also become an ongoing theme in a lot of our between-meeting conversations. I'll still pick up the phone some afternoons and call Andy, saying something like, "Hey, guess who just called and invited me to help him launch his new show in New York? Yeah, Robin Williams!" And so on.

Ironically, I actually did receive an email from a famous celebrity asking for insights into a T-shirt business he and his wife wanted to start, and when I told Andy this, he thought I was still play-acting. "Wow, cool," he said. "Hey, why don't you come over for a barbeque I'm having with Jay-Z and Beyoncé right now." I protested, "*No*, Andy, so-and-so really wrote me—*really! Really-really!*" "Right, and don't forget to bring over the Grey Poupon, Mike. . . ."

The pretending is starting to become real. *Wow.*

Your Turn

Try this exercise on the following page: jot down a dream of yours that has *already* come true, along with some of the consequences its fruition has already had on your life. Then write down a dream of yours that *will* be coming true, along with some of its anticipated consequences. Share both dreams with a friend or cool family member (or your reflection in the mirror if you don't have anyone who understands this stuff), and speak of *both* dreams in the *past tense—as if they've already come true.* That's super important. Don't say, "This dream has come true, and this one will be coming true." Speak of *both* in the past tense. Then, have your friend or family member share his or her dreams with you *as if they've already come true*, and each of you can speak of one another's dreams as well.

This simple exercise is powerful because it's going to take you and your mind's eye to the other side of the fence. You're going to be creatively challenged to start thinking of nuances to your life that will be real considerations one day in the near future, and you'll be forced to speak about them as if they were present-day manifestations—as if they have already wonderfully and "magically" come to pass.

Acting Lessons

Dream already come true:	Positive consequences of its fruition:
Dream you anticipate coming true:	Anticipated positive consequences of its fruition:
Restate the latter in past tense, as if it has already come true:	
I have already:	

6

Opening the Floodgates

In the opening chapter, I shared with you what I believe is the number one thing that keeps people from living their dreams: misunderstanding the nature of our reality. Second to that would be not taking action—the baby steps we've already talked about. And third, which I'm going to speak about in this chapter, is that so few people actually take into account their own extraordinary uniqueness when choosing from the paths that lie ahead of them, ignoring the beat of their own drummer. This third reason is what opening the floodgates is about: having the courage to follow your heart and to be yourself.

To Be (or Not to Be) Yourself

Being yourself sounds like it should be so easy to do—unless, perhaps, we've messed too long with the *cursed how*s or shoulds.

Football Heroes

I can recall when I was seventeen years old and growing up in St. Petersburg, Florida. On Sunday afternoons, one or more of the television networks would host a sports show featuring the highlights of the prior week's NFL super plays. And I mean *just* the plays that would take your breath away, one scene after another, back-to-back slow motion, with expert commentators describing each play. I always found myself *awed* by these hulking beasts—these modern-day gladiators—bursting down the field, sweat exploding off of their faces, as if they were performing some supernatural He-Man ballet. Gliding, floating, twisting, turning, throwing, catching. Fans going wild! Blood brothers unleashed to save all humanity! I'd be beside myself with anticipation as each play was relived.

The players' heroics and physical accomplishments were so glamorized I couldn't think of anything else in the hours, even days, after the show other than my sudden burning desire to become an American football hero. The power, the glory, the cheerleaders! Yet in my delirium and excitement, I'd conveniently forget that in my neighborhood my nickname was Butterfingers Dooley. I was forgetting that I could not catch a football with two hands, both feet planted firmly on the ground; forgetting that I was the slowest sprinter among all of my friends, with bowed legs that would go in every direction except forward; and, most conveniently, forgetting that, really and truly, I never liked playing football! But again, that didn't seem to matter because *I saw what I saw*, and it was easy to *completely forget who I really was*.

What Do You Want to Do?

My football story is exactly what I see playing out so often in life for others. Particularly with people who are new to understanding metaphysical principles and who, until recently, had spent most of their lives messing with the *cursed hows* (and some *cursed shoulds*, as well), to the point that they no longer know what they truly want to do. They see an inspiring film or read a self-improvement book and are suddenly saying things like, "Oh my gosh, Mike, this has changed my life! I could be the next Richard Branson. I could be the next Mick Jagger. I could be the next Tina Turner." The list of "coulds" or "shoulds" is endless.

But just because you like what Mick Jagger does onstage, or just because Betty down the road is selling lots of real estate, doesn't mean that you could or should be doing those things. *You can only be the next you.* Don't forget who *you* are. Now, of course, all things *are* possible; I'm not arguing that. But what I'm asking is, what floats *your* boat? What do you enjoy doing and what gets you excited about life? These are the billion-dollar questions. Your drummer is who you need to be listening to because when you do, as the saying goes, the money—*everything*—will indeed follow. Don't be swept off your feet with false motivators, whether it's messing with the *cursed hows*, fame and glory, or easy money. You must tune in to *yourself*.

Infinite Probabilities

This is what I see holding people back. False motivators are why people are tripping or stumbling, or spinning their wheels. People completely disregard their own inner makeup, their own preferences, their own desires, their own leanings and inclinations. Part of the explanation is that these folks, and it *could* be you (I know at times it's been me), confuse infinite *possibilities* with infinite *probabilities*. Big difference! Just because all things are possible does *not* mean that all things are equally likely or probable.

In fact, most things are extremely unlikely. For example, within the next three minutes, anything could happen in your life, right? You could close this book, you could do a little jig, climb a ladder, call a friend, change a light bulb; or maybe Martians will land in your backyard. You could begin speaking Urdu, or you might call a taxi for a long drive to your child-hood home. (You get the idea.) Yes, all things are possible, but what's likely?

Very, very, very few things are likely. Yet the one thing that has the greatest *probability* of happening in the next three minutes is your continued reading of this book. And after reading, there's an extremely high probability that you're going to do what you normally do at this time of day, give or take a few new possibilities that may already be on your radar. Tomorrow will unfold very much as it did seven days ago. Next week will generally follow this week. Although the fur-ther out in time, the less strong the probabilities, and even though all things remain *entirely* possible, the *probability* you'll eventually move to Madagascar is infinitesimal. This is a far cry from stating things are predetermined; they're not. But neither do infinite *possibilities* even remotely resemble infinite *probabilities*.

A Tidal Wave of Magnificence

Now let me back up and put this in an even broader context. Too often, people unaware of the truth of reality view themselves as a kind of "virgin soul." They think and act as if this is their first (and last) time in the jungles of time and space, when the truth of the matter is that you're an ancient, spiritual gladiator. You're a divine giant, and you've been rolling through the jungles of time and space like thunder for eternity.

When you got to this very time and space, you were a tidal wave of energy filled with desires, leanings, and inclinations. And it's this *enormous* wave of energy that meticulously and most brilliantly chose the stage on which you now live your life. By this lifetime, after riding your tidal wave throughout eternity, you knew *exactly* the kind of adventures that would electrify you. You knew exactly the kind of challenges that would help get you to the next level once they were faced. These are the reasons you're here now.

Therefore, in a very real manner of speaking, given the tidal wave of energy and intent that delivered you to this round of time and space, your life, *while still in your hands and entirely subject to your decisions,* comes somewhat pre-equipped with its own infinite *probabilities.* And when you now choose to *work within those probabilities,* which are simply a reflection of the greater and present-day you, you'll meet with less resistance, unleash greater synchronicities, and generally find success and happiness far more plentiful.

So to suddenly think, oh my gosh, I could be the next Lady Gaga, Donald Trump, or whoever, is to completely disregard *your* magnificence and all that brought you here. But to clarify again, I am not saying that these things are impossible, and I am not implying that the stage is set and can therefore be predicted; it can't.

One of the plainly evident facets of living in time and space is that we all have free will. Yet when you are choosing from the paths ahead that are *in line with your own extraordinary uniqueness (who—all—that you are), this is when the floodgates begin to tremble.* Suddenly, you're working within your own set of infinite probabilities, or far more simply stated, finally *just being yourself.*

Summoning Opportunities

Take a look at the "Infinite Possibilities" pie chart on the following page. If you were to put yourself in the center of that circle, you see there's a line going to the perimeter. That line represents one of an *infinite* of number of directions you could take with your life as you move outward from the center.

Now look at the second pie chart, called "Infinite Possibilities vs. Infinite Probabilities." The infinite probabilities slice is vastly smaller than that of infinite possibilities. It's meant to illustrate the realm of tantalizing *probabilities* that presently exist in this very life you are now living—filled with the kinds of adventures and challenges that led you to choose being you. When you work *within* this realm *by simply being yourself and doing the things that you most want to do*, everything starts "clicking." Working outside of this realm is like going against the current of who you are and all that's brought you here.

When you honor your own extraordinary uniqueness, opportunities suddenly come to you. And for every day, week, month, and year that you stay true to yourself, life gets easier and easier—to the point where you experience a momentous upward spiral of successes that begins gathering its *own* momentum. I can tell you that from where I am today, compared to my two prior and far less authentic careers, I have more people inviting me to participate in more things than I can even keep track of—socially, romantically, and financially. It's so much fun and, more important, *fulfilling* to be working

Infinite Possibilities

Infinite Possibilities

Infinite Possibilities vs. Infinite Probabilities

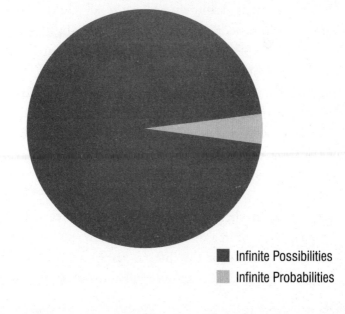

Infinite Possibilities
Infinite Probabilities

within my own realm of infinite probabilities. Not that my life is challenge-free. I still have my share of lessons to learn and expect I always will. As I said earlier, challenge is what makes an adventure an adventure. There will still be tricky days and growing pains, and to a lesser degree, fear. Yet, when you can grasp life's bigger picture, playing the victim becomes impossible and your rebounding skills become world class.

An Infinite Drop in an Infinite Sea

I can imagine that some of what I'm saying in this chapter may seem to imply that we're limited. After all, you can see that this subset of infinite probabilities is wildly smaller than the realm of infinite possibilities. In fact, the subset of probabilities for your life is most likely much smaller than what I (somewhat) arbitrarily drew compared to all that is *truly* infinitely possible. Nevertheless, this smaller subset represents your *infinite* probabilities. There is absolutely *no* limit to all you can do with your life, even while working within your "probability set."

For example, let's just say one of your natural leanings was toward teaching; you love working with people, and helping them learn and grow. So teaching is *just one* probability, and no doubt there are many other innate leanings you have. But let's look within that one little line of probabilities and see what some of the possibilities are.

If you love teaching, you would first have to answer, *How am I going to teach?* You could teach as I'm doing right now, by writing or maybe by speaking. You could teach face to face, by telephone, or in a studio making audio recordings. You could teach using video or the internet, or you could teach one on one. You might also teach more unconventionally, perhaps as a novelist, songwriter, or playwright. Ayn Rand, the naturalized Russian-American philosopher and novelist, taught her world-views through stories that she made up; she taught through fiction. You could be a radio disc jockey. Or you could teach like Bruce Springsteen who, while on stage before live audiences and between songs, tells stories laced with humor, morals, and calls to action. The *ways* you could be a teacher are truly infinite.

Then comes the bigger question: *what* are you going to teach? You could teach metaphysical thinking, biology, conservation, or mathematics. You could teach about the stars, the ocean, insects, or computers—the list goes on forever.

So, in this one little sliver of possibilities from within your range of infinite probabilities, you can see there are an *infinite* number of paths to follow just for teaching alone. And it's not as if we have only one little sliver of things that would resonate for us; there's a range wide enough to thrill and fulfill you for the rest of your life. This is the range to look for and identify with rather than thinking that you're some fungible commodity, like money, or some lump of clay, believing that everybody has an equal chance to succeed at either being a rock star, a politician, or an entrepreneur. *That* is simply not true. When you disregard all that makes you special, it takes away from your own brilliant magnificence—the very essence of you that makes you unlike anyone else. Just be *yourself*

The Courage to Be Yourself

Finding the courage to be yourself couldn't be easier. Yet if this seems like a struggle or is new thinking for you, or maybe you too have messed with the *cursed hows* or *shoulds* for far too long, perhaps your greatest challenge today is similar to what mine was ten years ago. I remember telling my brother after we liquidated our T-shirt and gift company that *if I only knew what I wanted to do, I'd be doing it.* I would sink my teeth into it. I would be like a pig in mud, and I'd never stop. *It would be my bliss.*

But I didn't know what I wanted to do. And if that's your situation, or if there are other concepts that are confusing you or preventing you from tuning in to your true nature, then let me give you a number of points or tips on having the courage to be (or to finally *discover*) yourself.

Be Led By Joy

One day this will be fun! Have you ever said that to yourself or someone else? Do not be led by the promise of future dividends. I think this was one of my major life lessons. The first time I learned the lesson of joy was playing competitive junior tennis. I started kind of late, at the age of thirteen, but I tried to catch up by practicing nonstop for hours on end. At first, it was a lot of fun, and I improved rapidly. But it quickly became a job—something I was no longer doing for fun but instead felt I *had* to do. Within a year, I *hated* playing tennis.

Rather than giving it a rest or doing something else, I rationalized that if I played *even more* every day, challenged more of my friends to play in matches at the club, and worked out longer on the backboard or on the court with a basket of balls to practice my serve, then *eventually* I'd start winning the tournaments, one day turn professional, and finally bring home some serious prize money. At which point—I continued rationalizing—I would really love playing tennis.

It didn't work, and it would *never* work. If you're going against your own grain, no matter how many hours you work; no matter how much blood, sweat, and tears are involved; it will never be a joyful endeavor. And this was most certainly true with tennis for me. I stuck with it for four more *years* and only became more bitter. When it became something I no longer enjoyed, the ability I had to improve was drastically diminished.

The same thing happened with public accounting. I did it because I thought it was what I *should* do, not for my love of numbers or the profession. I know this might sound a bit funny, like, who could love *that* profession, yet I was surrounded by brilliant and truly charismatic people—both our clients and my fellow workers. I learned that, unlike the stereotypical image most people have of accountants being bean counters working in a dimly lit back office wearing a visor, it is a profession that offers those who love it infinite avenues for creativity, growing a business, working on people skills, and improving efficiency and accuracy, among countless other skills. Yet even though I hold the utmost respect for PricewaterhouseCoopers and the friends I made there, and even though I managed to progress solidly through its ranks, by the time I finally resigned, I felt as though I was slowly dying from the inside out.

Finally, I again encountered this life lesson of *not being led by joy* when my mother, brother, and I liquidated what remained of our T-shirt and gift business. We each had enough money left over to financially coast for a couple of years, so I assessed my options. And at the time, they weren't pretty. I gave my attention to what I called *the least unattractive of my options* (yeah, a double negative, might need to read that twice!) because in truth, none of them looked that good. But I knew that I had to do *something*.

I had four choices before me. Option number one: I could polish off my old corporate accounting résumé and pound the pavement.

The second option was joining a brand new T-shirt company that I had just been made aware of, which seemed like a magical serendipity. As soon as we decided to close the doors of our business, I received an unexpected phone call from a long-lost friend who said that he wanted to start his own T-shirt company. Wow, what a "coincidence." But I would caution you: just because something seems amazing or serendipitous at first does not mean that this something "is meant to be." Naturally though, the opportunity seemed very fortuitously timed. I'd be joining a brand new start-up company with a quarter of a million dollars being invested by others as seed money. After talking with my friend and the other investors about how we might launch, there was one thing we were absolutely convinced of: we were all about to become fabulously wealthy!

The third option I had, of course, was to keep writing for tut.com—sending out my weekly emails and developing a website to support them, yet with no idea of how I'd ever "get any water out of that rock."

And option number four was irrigation repair. Yeah, I can't explain it, but I *love* irrigation repair. I remember fixing my own home's irrigation when I moved into the house I bought in 1994 and then going to the common area of my homeowners association and fixing all of their irrigation there *gratis*—as if it were my hobby. And it thrilled me! I don't know if it was the PVC, the elbows, the pop-ups, the rotors, or the glue, but I loved irrigation repair, and at this new point in my life, I was looking at all options.

Those were my four choices, but *not one of them offered the life of my dreams*. This could be where you are now. Oftentimes in life, we can't find anything that resembles a yellow brick road. But rather than do nothing, assess your options and, if none of them look particularly attractive, categorize them according to their standing as the *least unattractive*. This will give you *something* to do and some doors to knock on so that you will then be within reach of the Universe and life's magic.

As for me, I was going to knock on all four of these doors, or at least that was my intention. I polished off my résumé and sent it off to the corporate and accounting worlds, and *no one* showed *any* interest. I was totally shocked but comforted since it hadn't felt right anyway.

When it came to the new T-shirt business, after getting really excited about it (but *before* committing to it), I woke up one morning overcome with dread: I didn't want to get back into the T-shirt business, and I didn't care *how* much money I was going to make. This was a monumental turning point in my life, and I withdrew myself from consideration as a partner.

Then I turned my attention to tut.com and my writing. Happily, both took off. The writing success astounded *me* more than anyone else, and I loved this form of creativity. I then coupled my writing with expanding the website, launching TUT's Adventurers Club, and speaking on the same subjects that I wrote about: life, dreams, and happiness, which eventually turned into world tours, and our meeting here and now through this book.

I never did get to pursue the irrigation repair business, but a funny thing happened. About two years after tut.com took off, I was invited to a friend's new "palace" in a private, very exclusive gated community. Behind the gates of this community there were only fourteen homes, every one of them a mansion. One was especially big, about twice as large as all of the others. I could not help asking my friend, "Who the heck lives in that house, and what do they do?" "Oh, that's Larry Johansson, they call him the King ... of Florida Irrigation." *I knew it!*

And truly, you should know it, too. Abundance and fulfillment can lie down any path you choose, especially when choosing within your realm of infinite probabilities, whether it's irrigation repair, cleaning houses, or creative writing. So choose the path that excites and thrills you *the most*, not necessarily the logical one. The bottom line is not to be led by future dividends, even if this means choosing from the *least unattractive* of the options before you today. Find what resonates the most with the real you and then get busy. The next thing you know, as you start moving and the Universe responds in kind, whether it's weeks or months, maybe even years, the day *will* dawn when, I guarantee, you'll wake up and ask the same question I asked myself once the tide finally turned in my direction: "Wow, how did I ever get to be doing *this* for a living?" Be led by joy *now*, not future dividends.

Joy Doesn't Mean Challenge-less

Many people who are newly invigorated by metaphysical thinking conclude that living in joy means that they're going to be tiptoeing through life's tulips without any challenge or fear forevermore. Nope. Again, if your life didn't have challenges it would not be worth living. For this you're going to have to do your own deductive reasoning; this is a tangent that I'll let you follow on your own. But if your life did not have challenges, there would be no adventure. How much fun would it be to win the lottery every single weekend? It wouldn't!

Our challenges give our lives meaning; they help us rise to another level of enlightenment and understanding. Therefore, if you think you've figured out which path you'd like to go down in life (because it resonates in your heart) but suddenly see a lion, tiger, or bear standing before you one day, this doesn't mean it's the wrong path! Actually, it should probably confirm that it's the *right* one! It's almost as if our challenges show up by design: you pick something you want to do, and then you quickly realize that obtaining it is going to require you to be more than you've ever been before. *Awesome!* Keep going!

After I discovered how much I loved creative writing, especially on the nature of our reality, it dawned on me that one day somebody was going to ask me to talk to an audience about my passion, and just that thought gave me butterflies in my stomach. Shortly thereafter, I can remember looking up into the sky at airplanes flying over and thinking, "My gosh, one day I might be a speaker, and I might have to fly to get there." And *that* thought gave me more of the same butterflies.

I could have easily invoked my spiritual rights and said, "Hey, my *thoughts become things*, and the Universe conspires on my behalf. I don't have to go down that path if it scares me." But there was a greater voice inside of me (Old Faithful) that said, "Mike, you love talking on the nature of reality with

155

family and friends, and you love writing about it. Plus, you need to consider every possibility for increasing your cash flow. So how about you get over this irrational, ridiculous fear of speaking to larger audiences." This is when I joined Toastmasters. And although it took *many years* to get past the majority of the fear, public speaking and traveling the world to do it are now how I have the most fun in my life.

Incidentally, it's not my wish at all to be talking so much about myself. But I've found that when I share with audiences how scared and lost I was, as well as how I apply to my life all the methods I now teach to live wildly better, they can instantly find parallels in their life. And this then creates their own starting points for change.

Selfishness Is a Virtue

I'm going to throw you another curve ball: selfishness *is* a virtue. Too often, people confuse thoughtlessness with selfishness, yet thoughtlessness *can* exist independently. (That definitely doesn't sound like a very spiritual insight, but I hold to it.) If someone is trying to make gains for themselves in their life, or increase their own happiness at the expense of loved ones or those near to them, that's just thoughtless. How happy can they ultimately be if it comes at the expense, disappointment, or fury of loved ones?

True selfishness automatically takes into account the desires, preferences, and concerns of those in your immediate family and perhaps those in your immediate circle of friends and begins with taking the measures that consider all of the above. Not to the exclusion of following your own heart, but when considering all your options, there is almost always a happy medium that takes into account both your short- *and* long-term desires to be happy. And this inevitably means you'd also want to see smiles on the faces of those you care most about.

As Richard Bach said in his book *Illusions*, "Anyone who has ever given anything meaningful to the world has been a divinely selfish soul." And this is the context in which I mean selfishness is a virtue. *You must consider your own desires and preferences when choosing the paths before you.*

A Note from the Universe

This is to remind all my loyal subjects that you are not my loyal subjects. And that I'm bloody tired of all the sacrifices, appeasements, and groveling. I, the Universe—the sun, the moon, and the stars; the alpha and the omega and all the rest— have created a paradise in time and space so that I, through you, might experience its infinite splendors; drink from its every cup; and live, love, and be merry in ways impossible without you.

Your desires are my desires for you. What you want and when you want it—these were my ideas too; your dreams are my dreams. You are the be-all and end-all of time and space, the only reason for this Garden of Eden; you can do no wrong.

There are no mistakes, and it is all good. Follow your heart and delight in your preferences. Approve of yourself. Stake your claim— demand it—and hold out your hands. Banish your doubts, get off your knees, and live as you please because, dearest, you can, and this is all I ever wanted.

With unspeakable love, I am—
The Universe

Your Dreams Are Untouchable by Others

Do not worry that someone might keep you from your dreams. This is one of the most frequently raised concerns when I do a workshop or lecture, usually with people speaking generally and in somewhat veiled terms because they don't want to offend the spouse that they brought with them. They'll say such things as, "What if one person believes in *thoughts becoming things*—that we are spiritual beings and the Universe conspires on our behalf—yet the other person in the relationship doesn't? What if they think it's just a bunch of bunk, wishy-washy fairy tales?" You needn't worry.

There is no one who can keep you from happiness. There's no one who can make you sick. There's no one who can keep you lonely. There's no one who can keep you from abundance or fulfilling work. *No one.* Your dreams are untouchable, just as everyone else's dreams are untouchable. Otherwise, we'd be little more than puppets, and our free will would come with caveats.

Of course, there could be a situation where a couple has different ideas about where they want to live, for example. Maybe one wants to live in California and the other wants to live in Florida. Compromises are going to have to be made. But in your life's most sacred areas like happiness, health, or lifestyle, you are untouchable. So let people laugh at what you're doing. Let them have *their* beliefs while you remain true to yours, and be fearless with regard to the fallacy that anyone could possibly stop you from carving out your own amazing, wonderful life.

Your Life "Purpose" Is Simply to Be Yourself

If you're breathing, you're living your life purpose! Stop searching. Chill out and have fun. People often wonder, somewhat understandably, what their special niche is—that place they can uniquely fill which was made for them and only them; their reason for being; their "purpose." So I say again: as long as you're breathing, you're filling that niche. No one else can be, do, or see the things you can be, do, or see, and moreover, no one else ever has or ever *will* experience the feelings that are unique to *your* life and *your* adventure. If you're here, you're already filling that special niche.

Your purpose has no more to do with your chosen profession than the clothes you select to wear or the food you choose to eat. Whether you're a cook, banker, or pet sitter, it makes no difference. You came here to be happy, to learn and grow, and to thrive, and it's your prerogative to meet these ends any way that you want.

The purpose behind the lesson: do what you most want to do. Don't confuse yourself by thinking there's a predetermined niche that needs to be found by some predetermined path, all of which could sideline your action steps with doubt and timidity. You're not here to save the world. In fact, even if that were what you most wanted to do, the very best way to approach it would be to follow your heart and find your own happiness.

When Completely Stuck, Chance the Unknown

This advice to *chance the unknown* requires two things: (1) you're *really* stuck, meaning that you have absolutely no idea what you want to do with the rest of your life, and nothing I've shared so far is particularly helpful; and (2) you've got that internal, green-light indicator saying, "Hey, I could handle some huge life changes right now, *and* I could make them without jeopardizing my present responsibilities." If those two criteria are met, then consider *chancing the unknown*. And by this, I mean consider making a major life change—moving to a new city, state, or country; going back to school; or changing your career. Assuming you've got that inner green light and you're not going to be burning down bridges in your immediate circle, take that big leap. By making such a huge life change, you *exponentially* increase the opportunity the Universe will have to reach into your life, make adjustments, and show you new possibilities.

A Note from the Universe

Having preferences doesn't mean you're judgmental, whether they're likes or dislikes.

They just ensure that as the winds of divinity are blown through your heart, the melody is unlike any other.

So have them; have them big time.

You rock,
The Universe

PS—Like that one? Or dislike?

Honor Your Preferences

If you don't honor your preferences, then who will? No one else can know what stirs in your heart, what latent gifts you've yet to unwrap, or what your inner voice has been whispering to you all along. Our greatest responsibility in life is to be true to ourselves, and this means respecting your likes and dislikes; your preferences make you special. They're not cause for alarm but for celebration. Whether it is hip-hop music, tall people, blondes, or night work; or if you're drawn in any particular direction; honor it without criticizing yourself! Go where you're drawn, whether it's to country music, old Europe, bodybuilders, or flower arranging.

You're not here to fall in love with everybody or to win a popularity contest. You're here to fall in love with *yourself*. And from there, falling in love with others becomes effortless.

You Can Do This!

Here's a little exercise that you might consider doing right now. (There is space on the next page for you to work.) To begin, think of the things you love most about *life in general*—friends, travel, yoga, children, the ocean? Make a list of at least three things.

Now jot down what you love most about *being you*—your thoughts, sense of humor, body, and so forth.

Finally, write down the three most important life lessons you'd like to master in this lifetime. What are they? Finding courage? Practicing patience? Gaining self-confidence? Being funny? Having great relationships? Creating abundance? Living in the moment? Finding a fulfilling career? What would you like to master this time around?

First of all, assuming you've got these lists together, you've just revealed *why you're here*! This is it—your purpose, if you will. There are things you love about life and yourself, and there are things you'd love to master.

WHAT ARE THE THREE THINGS YOU LOVE MOST ABOUT LIFE, GENERALLY SPEAKING?

1.
2.
3.
Use extra paper to make this list much longer when you have time.

WHAT ARE THE THREE THINGS YOU LOVE MOST ABOUT YOURSELF?

1.
2.
3.
Use extra paper to make this list much longer when you have time.

WHAT ARE THE THREE MOST IMPORTANT LIFE LESSONS YOU'D LIKE TO MASTER?

1.
2.
3.
Use extra paper to make this list much longer when you have time.

Secondly, let the "hat" you wear at work and the baby steps you take in life be as reflective as possible of these lists. I realize you still may not know exactly what you want to do next or what you want to claim as the life of your dreams. But at least when considering your options, you can take into account what you just learned from this exercise. Considering your own extraordinary uniqueness can at least give you something to go on; doing something—*anything*—is always better than doing nothing. This is how you can start on step two of the miraculous mechanics of manifestation, moving in the general direction of your dreams—by taking inventory, if you will, on who you are, what you love and how you'd like to grow.

Remember that there's a hidden upside to working within your own set of infinite probabilities. Not only will you be choosing from choices that come as close as possible to resonating with you, but by finally taking action in a direction that considers who you *really* are, the floodgates *will* begin quaking! This is precisely when gigantic wheels begin turning behind the curtains of time and space in your favor. This is when legions are summoned to your assistance. This is when opportunities begin presenting themselves to you in wave upon wave of happy accidents, coincidences, and serendipities.

Life becomes what you've always wanted it to be: when you begin honoring (or at least attempting to discover) your own extraordinary uniqueness and when you have the courage to follow your heart—even when the first steps you take are neither glamorous nor sexy and are the least of your unattractive options. Please give this some thought because, as I said at the outset, this is one of the areas—if not *the* area for some—in which I too often see people kidding themselves, fooling themselves, and holding themselves back. You are the captain of your own ship, and there's nothing but a glorious horizon ahead.

7

Understanding Adversity

Understanding adversity, as I'm about to cover it, may challenge you, but as I said earlier, if questions remain on your canvas of understanding about the nature of reality, even when it comes to understanding the bad and the ugly, there goes your power. If we wish to deliberately exercise our divine powers, it becomes our responsibility to ask the hard questions.

Generally speaking, life is knowable—in the sense of how things work, why we are here, and what we can do with our time in space. It's logical, intuitive, and filled with meaning. And though we may not grasp its every nuance in the moment, we can still sense its order and perfection.

Why Does Bad Stuff Happen?

In spite of our ability to sense life's order and perfection, I used to wonder at length (and maybe you still do as well): "Why does bad stuff happen—why, in this Garden of Eden, this bastion of perfection, where otherwise we see such order, love, and splendor?" All you have to do is turn on the news and see that it's filled with nightmare stories of one person violating another, animals suffering, and more. It's enough to make your head spin.

A New Paradigm

One day, I was agonizing over the question of why bad things had to happen until suddenly, as has always been true when I dwell on something long enough, "a light went on." I got the answer, but I warn you that, at first read, it may seem horribly naïve. The answer is: bad stuff does *not* happen in time and space. The question itself is fatally flawed; it *presumes* that bad stuff happens. It only *appears* that bad stuff happens when you're so close to the occurrence that you're actually seeing it out of context.

I'm not saying that within the illusions of time and space, horrible, hideous, and disgusting things don't happen; they do! I'm also not saying there's no such thing as pain, suffering, or people bent on doing evil things. I *am* saying that there is far more to every such occurrence than we can grasp with our physical senses alone. I'm saying that if you stand back far enough from any situation, striving for as big a picture as possible, no matter what has happened, you will always discover purpose, meaning, healing, and love.

Contradictions Do Not Exist

Before I explain further, let me add that, for me, the idea that bad things don't happen makes sense. Of course, the concept raises gigantic questions at first, and I'll soon address those, but does it make sense that bad things *would* be happening in the magnificence of creation, God's paradise, this playground of Divine Intelligence? For me it doesn't. It doesn't make sense that there could be such sophistication among such complexity and love—a degree to which the human mind cannot begin to fathom—while simultaneously there would be vile, hideous, disgusting things. Thinking otherwise is like thinking God has made some kind of mistake, either in creating the cosmos or in deciding to create humans, who, unforeseeably *to God*, turned out to be a runaway train of badness. The latter idea, of course, completely negates what we confidently deduced in chapter 1—that we are pure God.

Ayn Rand wrote this about the nature of reality: "Contradictions do not exist. Whenever you think you are facing a contradiction, check your premises. You will find that one of them is wrong."

Let this apparent contradiction of bad stuff happening in an otherwise perfect world tip you off that there is a bigger, deeper, greater answer. And that answer begins with this: when you are far enough away from an experience to see it in a larger context—from a whole new paradigm—bad things do not happen in time and space.

Cancer

I've had the great privilege of meeting many cancer survivors, and almost every last one of them has told me, shocking me at first, that cancer was among the greatest *gifts* of their entire life. Gifts?! Now, close up, were they talking about the invasive disease that was destroying their very cells? Of course not! That's taking it out of context. They were talking about the *overall* experience and how they grew from it.

Healing irreconcilable differences

I realize that every cancer case is different and that there are as many reasons and hidden intents that give rise to cancer as there are people who've experienced it, but in some situations, cancer (or any disease) can, for example, bring family members and/or friends together who had previously been estranged—relationships that had previously been irreconcilable. In such cases, once the cancer is beaten, the love and friendships remain—love and friendships that perhaps could not have existed under other circumstances. For these people, was cancer a curse or a blessing? They've told me it was a blessing.

Enhancing appreciation

I've met many people who feel that their life has been such a struggle and their circumstances so "unfair"; they'll tell me, "If reincarnation exists, and if we have a say in the matter, *I'm not coming back*. This is it. I've had my fill." Hypothetically, however, if a doctor tells such a person that he or she has got, say, twelve more months to live, it's amazing how suddenly these people, having just been handed a virtual death sentence, find that their coffee in the morning tastes richer, bolder, and more wonderful than ever before. Some have told me they gained a new appreciation for a sunrise and a sunset—that the simplest things now rock their world. Take cancer out of the equation once they've beaten it, and the appreciation remains. For these people, was cancer a curse or a blessing? They've told me it was a blessing.

Discovering your power

Now consider the person who feels incapable of manifesting change in their life. They feel as though nobody listens to them; they feel absolutely powerless and depressed. You give such a person a terminal diagnosis from a doctor and suddenly they're waging an internal war for survival. With victory over an often-fatal disease, they're suddenly left with a newly found

MANIFESTING CHANGE

power—one which can now be used externally in the world around them from that point forward in their life. It is a power that they felt they lacked up until this point, but beating an "incurable" disease showed them otherwise. For these people, was cancer a curse or a blessing?

When you stand far enough back from *any* circumstance, you'll see the entire experience in context, and accordingly, you'll then see purpose, meaning, healing, and love.

Everyone beats cancer!

And what of the cancer patients I didn't get to meet, who succumbed to the disease and died? What would they have told me? Exactly the same thing. First off, from the larger perspective, they're not dead! You already know that when one door closes, another one flies open. They're all as alive now as they were in their bodies, and their adventures in thought will continue forevermore. From this perspective, *everyone beats cancer*! Yet for their own reasons, their time to physically check out had arrived. They were *ready* to move beyond time and space and from the highest within themselves, they *chose* the means for departing that would give them and those affected the greatest gifts. They knew what they were doing.

Blame-the-Victim Mentality?

This raises another question that I've heard from the media and from some participants in my programs: the question of fault or blame. People say, "Well, I can understand *thoughts become things*. And I can grasp the law of attraction. But doesn't that mean if something unpleasant happens to someone that they are to blame, that it's their fault?" This is sometimes

169

known as a "blame the victim" mentality, which I've been accused of having on occasion. But words like "blame" and "victim," when used by others, immediately presume things that I do not presume. We are creators—sparks of Divine Intelligence—here to taste the bounty of our own creativity; we are here to see, learn, and become proficient at deciding what happens in our private corners of time and space. Is it a young child's fault if, while learning to walk, he or she takes a tumble or two? Are they to blame? Or is the use of fault and blame here taking things out of context? Similarly, the "victim" label is never appropriate when spiritually explaining causes and effects in time and space.

People experience cancer, AIDS, and other diseases for their own purposes and intents, and such experiences impart lessons to the patient and others near them, including the discovery of their own power, an enhanced appreciation for life's magnificence, the capacity to forgive—the list is endless. This is *not* to say that at times there aren't unintended consequences to some of the decisions we make or the focuses we've chosen, but these all stem from our greater, entirely deliberate choice to be alive among the sometimes tricky, always enriching illusions of time and space. Whether intended or not, *everything* that happens on our journey adds to our wisdom and glory.

Children and Their Thoughts

Along these lines, I'm also asked about the suffering of children—those who are violated or perhaps murdered, before their life has even begun. To begin with, as I said earlier, there's the false presumption that we all enter the world as brand new souls and therefore with no choice in the matter. Yet if you can grasp that we are eternal beings and that time is an illusion springing from a greater reality, then doesn't it become obvious that just as we are eternal on a timeline stretching into infinity, so are we eternally stretching backwards on that same timeline? And if you can see this, then you realize all of us have lived before our lifetimes here began, and therefore that it was through our own choices that we are here now.

Then the question comes up that if we all lived before, where was "everyone" when Earth's population was only a few hundred thousand people, compared to today's nearly seven billion? But this question implies that not only must everyone live sequential lives without pauses in between, but that there's only one time-space world on one timeline and that everyone must be here at the same time! There are infinite worlds, infinite timelines, and perhaps an infinite number of potential "personalities" that never even choose to experience time and space.

Back to the point, children are not brand new souls; we are all ancient, adventure-loving gladiators who rode into time and space knowing full well the settings of the stage that we chose in each lifetime, and with brilliant reasons for choosing as we did. Some know that they might have a short lifetime, yet never has the length of a life been directly proportional to its quality. Moreover, with eternity as the backdrop from which we come and go, the duration of any lifetime becomes hugely secondary to all else. What matters most is the adventure itself, and *the ultimate adventure is always the one that leads us to love.*

Why might a life be chosen that could end abruptly in violence? Well, with nothing to lose, since we're eternal beings, the answer must lie in either the adventure that life would give us or the adventure it would make possible for others. Perhaps we allow ourselves to live on a stage where we *might* be violated if it creates circumstances in which the perpetrator *finally* understands the grotesque folly of their ways, and at last begins healing. Or perhaps we allow ourselves to stray into harm's way so that others might not "have to." Maybe we choose it to help others and ourselves to understand the mental anguish that often leads to, and comes from, violence. Or perhaps it would be for the shocking "wake-up call" it would provide to witnesses and to those distantly aware of what happened, so that they might pay closer attention to their own thoughts, words, actions, and resulting consequences. The reasons, including for the love of all involved, are endless.

The Littlest Heroes

Because the explanations just given go against everything we've ever been taught as well as all that our physical senses show us about how our lives unfold, let's drill down into a hypothetical example: Let's say that you have an ancient "soul friend" and the two of you are deeply in love—a love deeper than anything you've ever experienced in this lifetime. You have lived lifetime after lifetime together, frolicking in the jungles of time and space, loving the same kind of adventures, and learning the same kind of lessons until your best friend begins going down a few paths without you. These paths hold absolutely *no* interest for you, and although they obviously appealed to your friend at one point, over time they have left him confused, disoriented, and afraid—*very* afraid. You're horrified because, life after life, his confusion grows to the point that he doesn't even *recognize* you anymore. And worse, you see that he begins resorting to anger, rage, and violence as a means to combat his fear; as a coping mechanism to deal with the terror he now perpetually feels. *And you want nothing more than to help.*

For this desire of yours to be of service, to help spark his healing and recovery, let's say that it's then shown to you that you *could* help by being a child of his in an upcoming life. You're also shown that, should you choose this, at the moment of your birth, when your eyes first meet as child and parent, there will be a spark of recognition—a connection—and a powerful surge of love between you, although neither of you will know exactly what it means. Nonetheless, it will be a surge so great, that your long-lost friend wouldn't have felt anything remotely like it in many, many lifetimes.

It's also shown to you that even if you make this choice, your friend will still be terrified by his life and prone to continued fits of rage and violence. Some of this violence might even be directed squarely at you. You see, however, that should your friend hurt his only beloved (you), he will finally understand the destructive nature of his behavior, leading to a long-overdue realization that anger and violence are never a solution and only make matters worse. Then—and only then—will your friend's healing take off at warp speed.

If this was the case (hypothetically), and you were given the opportunity to reach out and be a lifeline, would you volunteer? Would you accept the assignment? I think you would, *especially* since you'd be presented with this option from the zenith of your awareness, fully seeing the entire spectrum of reality, with total understanding of life's beauty and your eternal being. Grasping that you'd have *absolutely nothing* to lose, you see that you could live yet another seven trillion lifetimes if you wanted to. And knowing of the immense potential for gain that may come from such a choice.

Now of course, it would be a choice and you wouldn't *have* to participate. But if you didn't, you'd have to agree with me that if your friend proceeded with that lifetime, and if there was the violation of another child, it would be because *someone else* had volunteered. Someone else *would have had to* offer to be that lifeline because the alternative is to believe that such a violation was a random accident. And such an alternative trashes almost all of the other deductions we reached in chapter 1, which would totally negate that thought forms matter and that we are spiritual beings who create our own realities.

With Understanding Comes Power

This is very heavy material, but again, I want to erase any and all question marks you still have from the tapestry of your life's understandings. I'm trying to explain something; *I am not justifying it*, just as a doctor who explains AIDS or cancer is not justifying these diseases. But by explaining them, they're educating and empowering those who hear their message, which is my greatest hope for what I teach.

Furthermore, my explanations don't remotely imply that we shouldn't help those who have suffered at the hands of others. Sometimes people choose "adversity" partly to spark awareness in bystanders. And suddenly, in these bystander's hearts, there's an awakening of compassion and empathy to reach out not only to the one suffering but also to others they love or had ignored before.

Nothing is by chance, nothing is random; there is always meaning, purpose, healing, and love. I don't want to go off on too much of a tangent here, so I invite you to visit the

"Ask Mike" section of the tut.com website if these kinds of insights interest or trouble you. There's probably been over a hundred questions asked that I've responded to on the site, many of them pertaining to war, catastrophe, and suicide, in addition to those concerning happiness, love, and manifesting change. In particular, you'll see that there's one section called "War and Disasters." If you click through on the "Tsunami" link, I talk about how we can grasp the mechanics of mass events, such as the 2004 Indian Ocean tsunami or the 2010 Haiti earthquake.

With understanding, you need not go through life thinking that bad things happen to good people. While that belief may seem comforting at times, it's just a temporary band-aid keeping you from seeing the overall picture of life's magnificence and from discovering your full power.

A Note from the Universe

*To those who ask why bad stuff happens in a
magical world with a loving Universe, I ask, does it?*

*Why do so many in time and space draw conclusions
based upon the perceptions of their physical senses alone?
As if your physical senses have ever been useful in explaining
the ethereal. As if there could have somehow been a mistake.
And as if they haven't yet grasped, based upon
the effortless possession of their own,
that life must be eternal.*

*Yeah, "Wow . . ."
The Universe*

Depression and Unpleasant Emotions

Let's talk about something else that we're all familiar with: depression and other wobbly emotions, like feeling disconnected to the world around you, out of the loop, powerless, dependent, or homesick (even from the comfort of your own home). Have you felt any of those feelings in the last twelve months? In the last month? Yeah, perhaps in the last week or even today? And my message here is *it's okay.*

You'd be surprised (or maybe not) by how many people approach me with serious concerns about their mental state simply because they harbor some doubts, occasionally feel depressed, or can't seem to be "whoo-hoo" happy 24/7. Bumps in the road are par for the course—to be expected, given the magnitude of the adventure we've chosen. *Life's journey* is filled with challenges and is hardly a Sunday drive in the country. Not that anyone should wallow in their unpleasant emotions, which only perpetuates them, but chances are that you need to cut yourself some slack and avoid being too critical, and judgmental, or hard on yourself.

My friend, you are *not* flawed or broken—there is nothing wrong with you—simply because you're not yet living what you consider a "perfect, happy life." Such sad conclusions stem from the symptoms I just shared (the bumps in the road) and are as unfortunate as they are debilitating. *You are a one-of-a-kind gift from the Universe, to the Universe, and you are adored!* You deserve and have earned the right to lighten up and enjoy the ride.

A NOTE FROM THE UNIVERSE

You do know, of course, why you're here don't you?

Because you couldn't resist the challenge!

Nothing in all creation, not in any sphere of the universe, compares to being born into time and space without any recollection of your past. Having to find your own way when lost, your own courage when frightened, and the infinite powers at your disposal when challenged. Left to the elements to rediscover your supremacy over them.

Driven by your passions so that you might rise above your humble, naked beginnings and ultimately see through the illusions that have trapped you. To find yourself once again high upon the throne of thy kingdom come, from whence it all began.

Well, either that . . . or you were dared.

Walking on sunshine,
The Universe

I cannot grasp or conceive of an adventure more daring than the one you and I are now on. I read very little, but the books that I have read are invariably channeled, such as the *Conversations with God* volumes of Neale Donald Walsch and *The Seth Material* by Jane Roberts. In these and the other books, they talk about "angels," who are aware of our presence and surround us on planet Earth, yet who have never lived a lifetime in the illusions of time, space, and matter. And the authors say that these angels look at us, those who have taken this gigantic plunge into the illusions, *with total awe*. They revere us. They revere *you* for your virtually unimaginable courage to go where relatively few have ever gone before—to a place of forgetting your own magnificence and divinity so that you can rediscover it. To be renewed and empowered to a degree that will take you beyond where you started. Take this into consideration the next time you feel a little disconnected, homesick, or depressed, and do not start unfairly labeling yourself.

Moreover, just because you've got these internal conflicts from time to time, or even quite frequently, that doesn't mean you can't live the life you dream of living.

A NOTE FROM THE UNIVERSE

As if the most accomplished amongst you didn't have their own piercing doubts, fears, and worries. Didn't have spells when they believed they were inadequate, lost, and dependant. Hadn't at times felt downhearted, discouraged, and all alone in the world.

Yet still . . . you know their names.

You are no less,
The Universe

There's no one who's achieved *anything* or who's *ever* lived in time and space who hasn't also experienced the same kind of highs, lows, and emotions that you and I experience. This is no cause for alarm; just go back to the truth—the truth that you are a divine creator, that your *thoughts become things*—and from there, just do your best to keep in motion. It's like riding a bike: you can't stay on it if you're not moving forward. Of course, there are times when we need to rest—but never for too long.

That's *understanding adversity*. Yet, because you will experience both highs and lows, and ebbs and flows forevermore, let me share some ideas that may help you turn future "adversities" into future adventures.

Turning Adversity into Adventure

Accept Responsibility for Everything

Without *absolute* responsibility, there cannot be *absolute* power. In other words, without accepting responsibility *for absolutely everything in your life*, you will not have absolute power to change what displeases you. If you give away even 1 percent of your power, whether to a god you don't understand; to karma; to your spouse, parents, or kids; or even to the so-called "mysteries of life;" that 1 percent could threaten to undermine all of your hopes and dreams, effectively stealing 100 percent of your power. Get rid of this illusion by accepting full responsibility.

The trick

Here's something that will make this a lot easier: you do *not* have to explain something in order to accept responsibility for it. In fact, I advocate that you not even consider explaining those things that now pain or confuse you. Leave them for now and look forward. You don't have to explain why the relationship didn't work, why the business didn't take off, or why you were violated as a child in order to accept responsibility for any and all such puzzlements. Know, deep within, that there was meaning, intent, healing, and love behind it, and leave it for consideration when your emotions are not so sore. Accept that you had a role in its creation, however mysterious, and in that moment of accepting responsibility, your crown will be restored so you can begin deliberately moving forward, creating and choosing anew.

My biggest train crash?

When I look back ten years ago to what seemed like the train crash of my life career-wise, I can remember then that explaining it was beyond me. I also realized that if I started looking for what was "wrong" with me, oh man, I would have found a long list of things! Which would have led to labeling, condemning, and lowering my expectations with regard to what I could still aspire to. Instead, what worked for me (and may work for you), was not giving *any* thought to trying to explain what had just happened. Knowing even then how life worked, I decided upon my new end results (wealth and abundance; friends and laughter; creative fulfilling work; and international travel), and I began knocking on doors (taking action).

Two to three years into my new journey, once my life began purring again, out of simple human curiosity, I wondered, "Man, what happened back when I *thought* the train crashed?" But looking back over my shoulder, to my total amazement, I couldn't find any remnants of a crash. In actuality, and with hindsight, it became clear that there never was a train crash.

Before this episode in my life, I wrote about life, dreams and happiness, putting my insights on T-shirts that were also adorned with little fishies, dolphins, and whale tails, and were sold in souvenir markets. During this time, my biggest wish was to reach far more people with my "thoughts" than I could as a T-shirt slogan writer. Well, ever since that so-called "train crash," I've *still* been writing about life, dreams, and happiness—and now I reach a lot more people!

My work and teachings on the very same topics now stretch far beyond writing and encompass more than I ever imagined. It turns out the train of my life had only changed tracks ten years ago in response to a *greater* dream I had. In other words, it was the start of the biggest dream of my life (so far) coming true. Yet ten years ago, there was such a "noise and racket" from the changing of the tracks, it would have been easy to draw conclusions that something was very wrong with me, especially since I didn't have the perspective to see or understand what was really happening at the time. Fortunately, I knew enough to accept responsibility, thereby retaining my power, avoiding worry about figuring it out, and simultaneously setting new end results as I knocked on more doors.

Had I gone down the path thinking, "I'd better get to the bottom of this! I'd better figure out how I'm sabotaging myself," there's a good chance you and I would have never met as author and reader. If I had looked for what was "wrong" with me, I would have found limiting beliefs that would have then dragged into my future. Furthermore, nothing "bad" or undesirable had happened! I didn't lose any career momentum; I'm still doing the same thing to this very day that I was doing almost twenty years ago, just more on my own terms.

You don't have to explain where you are today because where you are today is never *who* you are. But by accepting responsibility for it—*full responsibility*—you'll be fully empowered to move forward.

Get Back in the Saddle and Ride

When it comes to turning adversity into adventure, one of the most empowering things anyone can do after being bucked off by life is to get back in the saddle and ride! Nothing will take your eye off a gloomy past or present quicker than casting your attention to the future. You've got the rest of your life ahead of you; don't wallow in self-pity. You may have earned the right to wallow, you may deserve to take some time off, and you may have been through "hell" by now, but beyond a few weeks or months, wallowing isn't going to serve you.

Losing a child and a spouse

One of my dearest friends in the world is a speaker in the United Kingdom who teaches this concept to the audiences she speaks to, corporate and public alike, and she knows what she's talking about from firsthand experience. Twenty years ago she received a phone call at work from the police department informing her that her only child, who was just four months old, had passed away while in the care of his babysitter—an unexplained crib death. Devastated, she took refuge in bed for weeks, overwhelmed with grief. Subsequently, her husband told her that he couldn't handle it anymore and that he was moving out.

Losing your livelihood and everything else

A short time later, living alone and barely back on her feet, attorneys unexpectedly knocked on her door one evening and asked if she was aware that the company she and her husband had started from scratch years earlier, which was by then grossing over $2 million a year in revenue, was actually bankrupt. They continued by telling her that it was just discovered that her husband had been embezzling money from the company to fund a failed, illicit massage services business he had secretly launched (the real reason he moved out).

The next year, her father passed away from brain cancer, and her mother died from an undiagnosed heart condition just two days after an emergency operation. In a relatively short span of time, she lost virtually everything and was literally living off the kindness of strangers.

Until one morning, something changed. Lying in bed and crying, still suffering from the loss of her son, she suddenly had the realization that she and her "lost" son would one day meet again and that they would have a conversation that would go one of two ways: He would either say, "Mom, I'm so sorry you lost everything! But I'm so proud of you. You turned it all around. You got back in the saddle and you rode! You held your light high enough to brighten the darkened paths of others who needed to know there was still hope in their own lives after experiencing their own heart-wrenching losses." Or, the conversation could go something like, "Oh Mom, I'm *so* very, very sorry . . . You weren't supposed to die when I died." She realized in that moment, on that morning, that the rest of her life was about the rest of her life.

On the grief scale, she had earned every right to stay in bed and cry. She had lost more than most of us could ever comprehend losing, yet she still had the choice to live the life she was still blessed to have.

Bad things do not happen in the grand scheme of life

Many years later she and I became friends, and she attended a talk I gave in Manchester, England, covering exactly the material contained in this book. When I got to the part on adversity, I shared her story with my stunned audience of several hundred and then asked her if she would concur that "bad things do not happen." She replied that while those were years of absolute horror and turmoil, they were also years filled with the greatest blessings she'd *ever* received. She now understands that she didn't lose her son, for they'll be together forever. Nor did she lose her parents, whose presence is only ever a thought away. On the other hand, she did lose what some might call (not me, of course) a jerk of a husband.

Moreover, she discovered a power within her as *she alone* fended for herself, which up until that point in her life she didn't even know she had. And that power now shines forth every single day of her life, personally and professionally, as the mother she later became, and as a professional speaker and corporate consultant.

Get back in the saddle and ride. No matter where you've been or might one day go, it will always remain a beautiful world, brimming with infinite possibilities for you to live the life that you'd most like to live.

Help Others

Little else offers a better insight on our own situations than helping others who want or need the same thing that we do. If it's more confidence you want, find someone who wants more confidence as well and help him or her find their own. If it's more abundance, help someone find abundance in his or her life. If it's creative, fulfilling work, give someone wanting the same an idea or two; hold their hand, and you will see yourself and your own situation in a brand new light.

I made a friend eight years ago when visiting Hawaii. He was in one of my audiences and subsequently invited me to speak to three or four different groups in Oahu. Over the course of a week, he and I became friends, played golf together, and he remains one of the most well-rounded, balanced individuals I have ever met. He runs an organization called United Self-Help of Hawaii, which provides self-help care and recovery programs for people afflicted with virtually every form of mental illness, including those with schizophrenia and former mental hospital residents to those dealing with severe depression, anxiety, and other more common ailments. Joining them in 1987, he rose through the ranks to become their director, helping people get back on their feet, find their own identity, discover their power, and live rewarding lives to the greatest degree possible.

By the end of our week together, I was absolutely stunned to discover that before his career began in Hawaii, he was considered mentally ill because he suffered from clinical depression. His ability to cope and the recovery that followed were made possible as soon as he reached out to others who needed the same kinds of services, assistance, and care. By helping others, he helped himself.

Today United Self-Help of Hawaii enables people dealing with mental illness to have access to free computers, golf lessons, surfing lessons, swimming lessons, and much more, all in exchange for their continued participation in recovery and care. He has achieved such great success with his programs that other states are now modeling some of their healthcare programs after the model he created.

Through helping others, you *always* inevitably help yourself.

Choose Perspectives Wisely

This is your ace in the hole, because if you can change your perspective you can change how you see and feel about the entire world.

A Note from the Universe

If you knew of a spectacular mountain that was very,
very tall, yet climbable. And if it was well-established
that from its peak, you could literally see all the love that
bathes the world, dance with the angels, and party with the gods.
Would you curse or celebrate each step you took
as you ascended it?

Righto!
Life is that mountain and each day a step.

Perspectives change everything,
The Universe

PS—Fear not. Last time I checked, you were so close to the top
they were taking your toga measurements.

You Can Do This!

This is another simple exercise, and its intent is clear: if a past challenge once made your life better, is there really such a thing as adversity? Using the work space on the right, list a past challenge and note how it has made your life better now. Once you've done that, list a challenge you have today and how it has, or will, make your life better.

No matter what the challenge, no matter what the hardship, no matter what the violation, when you stand far enough back from the equation, you will see that you do indeed live in paradise and that you've got the rest—or I should say, *the best*—of your life to look forward to.

A Past Challenge:

How experiencing this challenge made your life better:

A Present Challenge:

How experiencing this challenge *has* made or will make your life better:

A NOTE FROM THE UNIVERSE

I keep telling them that it's a jungle out there. That time and space isn't a place for scaredy-cats. That toes are stubbed, hearts are broken, and dreams can seem to be shattered into a million pieces. I tell them that the illusions are so captivating, they won't even remember who they really are. And that the emotions can be so painful at times, they may fleetingly wish they were dead!

But that just makes them want to go even more.

Adventurers, you bad . . . ,
The Universe

8

It's Your Turn

You've suffered enough. You've struggled enough. You've pined, you've yearned, you've dreamed enough. You've paid your dues, and it is time. *It's your turn. Your turn* to play on the stage of life. *Your turn* to live the life you've always wanted to live. *Your turn* to be the person you've always dreamed you'd one day be.

107,000,000,000

One hundred seven billion. Do you know what that number represents? Anthropologists have said it's roughly the total number of human beings to have *ever* graced the face of the Earth. The total number of hearts that have *ever* beaten, the total number of journeys that have *ever* been taken, and the total number of lives that have *ever* been lived in time and space. A hundred seven billion people, no two quite the same, yet with a little bit of thinking, I bet you can deduce what 100 billion of them have in common. Yep. They're dead. For them, one adventure has come to a close and another has begun.

But for the seven billion of us who are still here, *it's now our turn.* Our turn to laugh and cry, our turn to love and be loved, our turn to dream and to make those dreams come true—for just a little while longer. Of course, we are forever beings, but the chance to have the opportunities we have now, to have the opportunities *you* have now on this stage that you've meticulously crafted, will *never* come again.

This is an extraordinarily unique, precious, and rare opportunity—and it's yours. This is *your* life we're talking about, and you can do anything you'd like with the rest of it; *you have that power.* And the good news—the *phenomenally* good news—is that when it comes to manifesting change, *it couldn't be easier.*

The Need for Understanding
Quantum Physics—Not!

Now, I know one of the rages in metaphysical thinking these days is quantum physics. You probably saw the movie *What the Bleep Do We Know?* It's an outstanding film, and rather "fortuitously" it brought a lot of mainstream folks into the realization that life is not at all what we had heretofore thought it was, that the stage we play our lives upon is illusionary—that we influence and even create it, hinting at our ability to deliberately change the circumstances we live in. But let me advise that apart from your own curiosity, you needn't go any further down that path of quantum physics to affect meaningful life changes. You don't need to learn more than what is now stirring in your heart.

Creating life changes doesn't require a scientific background. It's so simple. *Thoughts become things!* Change your thoughts, change your life! In fact, all quantum physicists will tell you that their ultimate ambition is to arrive at one simple, unifying equation—as simple as Albert Einstein's $E=mc^2$.

They believe that an equation exists that will tie together *all things* physical *and* metaphysical.

Well, no doubt one day they're going to discover it. But do you know what your thoughts are going to be doing between now and that discovery? *Becoming the things and events of your life—unfailingly.* In fact, in my way of thinking, the equation they're looking for is *Thoughts Become Things*: TBT! And these were my exact thoughts when I penned the following Note:

A NOTE FROM THE UNIVERSE

By all means, quantum physics totally rocks.
Just don't let its search for the unifying equation of the
cosmos distract you from using it.

I mean, one needn't know trigonometry to use chopsticks, eh?
Gravity was gravity long before Newton, huh? And between now
and the time they reveal their little theorem, your thoughts
will unceasingly become things, as the entire world spins
in the palm of your hand.

Aren't we amazing?
The Universe

PS—Thoughts Become Things, *incidentally,*
is the equation they're looking for. But let's not ruin it for them
(scientists can be so grouchy).

Manifesting change simply hinges on you having a new end result in mind, dwelling upon that end result from time to time, imagining it, perhaps visualizing it, and then consistently taking action in its general direction, *vis-à-vis* the baby steps.

Fortune Favors the Bold

Have you ever heard the old expression "fortune favors the bold"? Doesn't that resonate with you? *Fortune favors the bold!* For me it definitely resonates, and I remember the first time I heard it; it evoked mental images of champions winning gold medals at the Olympics, tycoons amassing vast fortunes, and a *fifth* star being added to a military General's lapel for valor and conquest. *Fortune favors the bold.* I'd imagine it resonates to some degree for everyone, yet giving it even more thought, my interpretation of its power and meaning is now far different than what it once was.

Getting Started

With a little bit of thought, you can actually see that boldness *isn't* winning the marathon, it's *deciding to run* the marathon. Boldness isn't something that comes at the end of a journey; *it comes at its beginning.*

Think of Oprah Winfrey. Which was bolder: when she launched what is debatably the most beloved television network on the planet or when, as a young, undereducated, overweight African-American teenager, she decided to interview for a broadcasting position against older, more experienced, better-educated, thin, white men? The latter! *That* was bold. That was the kind of step that takes such audacity most people never take it. And that's *why* it was bold.

It's the baby steps that are bold, coupled with high expectations, because most people are so psyched out by the bling, the medals, and the accolades of their heroes and heroines that they've completely forgotten that these very people often started their journeys with much less than you and I have now!

How about Walt Disney? Which was bolder: when, as a multimillionaire in the 1950s, he purchased forty-three square miles of Central Florida wilderness or when he returned home from World War I, having been stationed in Germany, and announced to his friends and parents that he would be hanging up his fatigues so that he could follow a dream that would begin with becoming a cartoon animator at a time when *almost no one had ever been* a cartoon animator? Where could he possibly think animation would take him, especially back then? Yet as we now know, this is exactly what set his entire, brilliantly famous career into motion, from which generations of families around the world have been enriched. *That* was bold!

Or Mohammad Ali? Which was bolder: when he won one championship match after another after another or when he stepped into a boxing ring for the first time, not knowing if he would even walk out? Always, it's these baby steps that demonstrate true boldness. It's these baby steps that summon fortunes—*precisely because* at the time you take them they seem so incredibly futile.

Where Did Your Past Successes Actually Begin?

Most of us could not climb Mt. Everest tomorrow, but virtually everyone reading these words could *begin preparing* to climb Mt. Everest tomorrow. It's what you start now, today, that will demonstrate your boldness. Look at your own life for proof.

I look at mine and wonder which was bolder: when I announced World Tours 1, 2, or 3, which took me to six continents and twenty-five countries, or when, ten years ago at my first Toastmasters speech, with a quivering voice and knocking knees, I read a four-minute speech to fourteen strangers and shook like a leaf on a tree? Where did *I* get off thinking that that could take me anywhere in life? Speaking in spite of my fear was bolder.

By comparison, my world tours are now a cakewalk! Effortless. It gets easier and easier as you go because of the courage, determination, and boldness in those very first few baby steps. Hold on to your dream. Let the Universe have every opportunity to reach you. And while the big picture of manifesting change is indeed one of ease, in the very beginning of any new adventure, there will inevitably be some discomfort, effort, or anxiety. But this is no cause to turn and hightail it.

Understanding is what makes boldness possible, intuitively if not intellectually, and understanding is what I most want to convey to you here and now with this book about manifesting change. First, understand your magnificence—that you're an eternal gladiator of joy, a spiritual adventurer, a being of light. Then understand that all change comes about when you have a new end result, or a new thought, that you then *move* with. And fortune will favor you even when your steps are small, and even when they're not glamorous or sexy. In fact, rarely will they be either; rarely will they be anything at all to brag about.

A Note from the Universe

The one thing all famous authors, world-class athletes,
business tycoons, singers, actors, and celebrated achievers in
any field have in common is that they all began their journeys
when they were none of these things.

Yet still, they began their journeys.

You are so poised for greatness,
The Universe

PS—One day, they're going to name something big after you!
Like a statue, a college . . . or a hurricane.

Bon Voyage, Fellow Adventurer

You are an *effortless creator*. Revel in that fact; revel in the glory
and the magnificence and the truth of it, because the bottom
line is that no matter what you do with the rest of your life,
no matter how glorious and profound, it will never compare
to the fact that you're even here at all. You're already in the
winner's circle. You're *already* on the cutting edge of reality
creation, right now as you read these words. There is nothing
else you *have* to do. The title of this book, *Manifesting
Change*, like the similarly titled programs or books available
today, is not intended to imply that you're broken or incom-
plete. Everything is cool right now, *especially you*. It's already
all good.

Yet, if at any point in your life from this day forward
you'd like to deliberately manifest change, then it's my greatest

hope that I've given you some pointers and clarity on precisely how to do that. I trust that by now you will forevermore be able to peer over the "sunglasses" you've been wearing your entire life to see how life *really* is—to see that when it comes to manifesting change, it couldn't be easier than *getting what you think about.*

You could not be, nor will you ever be, more powerful than you already are. You couldn't be more beautiful than you already are. Give this to yourself as your starting point, and everything else will appear achievable.

You don't have to overly stretch or make difficult sacrifices. Work within your comfort zones. Work with what feels right for you. You'll quickly discover your own exciting set of infinite probabilities, and when moving within their realm, the floodgates will begin trembling, guaranteed. It's the law.

Breaking It All Down into Far Fewer Words

All you ever have to do to manifest change is define what you want in terms of the end result. The Universe will do all the calculations backwards from that destination, because in the instant you define what it is you want, the Universe knows the exact sequence of events necessary to get you from where you are today to this place you dream of being. But remember, that sequence will not be allowed to play itself out *until* you put "your car in gear"; and that's up to you. Take the baby steps, knock on doors, and turn over stones.

Finally, as I've cautioned before, do not judge the journey with your physical senses alone because it will look weird at best, and at worst you'll think nothing's happening and end up quitting. Don't quit. *Don't ever quit.* This system, this plan, this rationale is the truth. It always works. The Universe is just an extension of you; it's your greater self. And it is conspiring even now to give you what you most want.

Remember the Matrix. Take a look at it, think about it from time to time, and remember what really matters the most to you: happiness. It's not *how* you get to where you want to go, it's *getting to* where you want to go. And where you want to go is a place of sunshine, butterflies, and rainbows; a place of joy; a place where you have abundance, health, friends, creative and fulfilling work, and you radiate with pride over your fabulous appearance. It is easy. You can do it. You're virtually there; it's just beneath your nose. One day at a time, one step at a time. You have what it takes, and you've paid your dues.

You are deserving, and you are loved. And on top of all that, the Universe is on your team. *What could be better than having the all-wise, all-knowing, all-loving, compassionate Universe at your side?* Actually, there is something better . . .

A Note from the Universe

I have to tell you that one of the greatest things about being the Universe is knowing absolutely everything. Well, that and making dreams come true. I also love being eternal and having no limits, creating worlds simply with thought. Knowing that reality is unfolding just exactly as it should. Having it all, being it all, doing it all. And I like being perpetually in love and loved.

How about you?

What's your favorite thing about being the Universe?

197

You are,
The Universe

Are you beginning to see it? You *are* the Universe. You are the sun, the moon, and the stars. You are the energy that beats your heart and the dreams you entertain day and night. And you can live the life of your dreams on this plane of manifestation by moving with your vision.

Every day brings you more opportunities to smile, to fall in love, and to feel fulfilled. Every single path before you will lead you to the life of your wildest dreams. You can't choose incorrectly—*unless you don't choose!* Nothing you have ever done, and nothing you will *ever* do, can take one moment away from eternity. *You cannot fail.*

Guided Visualization for the Days Ahead

Before we get to the pop quiz—yes, there's a pop quiz (I promise, it's short)—I want to walk you through a guided visualization to give you something else to think about in the days ahead and to help you truly sense all that you have to look forward to.

Imagine you're at the beach. You're sitting on a veranda attached to a magnificent beach house and right now you can hear the surf crashing . . . You can smell the salt in the air . . . and you can hear the occasional seagull calling out to others . . .

The sun is setting, and you've got a huge smile on your face. Go ahead and smile. You're beaming with joy because the house behind you is filled with all of the people you love the most. You're feeling so much joy that a tear trickles down your face as you relish why these dear friends have gathered. Each is there because they love you ... as much as you love them. And they're there to help you celebrate all of the fantastic changes that have been sweeping through your life. Changes that have shocked and amazed you, as much as them, with their speed and harmony.

Deeply grateful, you make a promise to yourself while still sitting on the veranda that never again, for the rest of your life, will you ever let yourself forget how swiftly things can change for the better! Right now, it's as if, in your life, every cup is overflowing: there's abundance, you love your life, you love your work, you're creatively fulfilled. You've never had so many friends, and you've never laughed so hard. Virtually everything you've ever wished for has come to pass ... With one tiny exception—there's one cup not yet overflowing

The one thing now missing in your life has come in the form of a brand new desire. You now wish with every fiber of your body to impart the joy you're feeling—the fulfillment and the love—to all those you so love. And not stopping there, you wish you could give these feelings to everyone in the world. Everyone on planet Earth should feel as good as you now feel, should be as loved as you are now loved, should have as much going on in their life and as many dreams coming true as you now have in your life.

But you can't. You feel limited. Briefly disappointed to the point of losing your smile ... until suddenly, as if struck by lightning, spontaneous illumination arrives and you remember that it was not that long ago when you were bobbing high and low in the troughs of life. When you were frustrated, when you were spinning your wheels. Yet, it's now obvious to you that your place on the veranda, right here and now, with this joy you've been feeling was always . . . inevitable.

And suddenly, there's another flash of insight! Now you realize that you needed to go through all you went through, everything in your life, to be at this magnificent place of realization and deep understanding. And you see that just as it was ultimately inevitable for you to get to this point, so is this true for all of those you love and for everyone now on Earth. This realization overwhelms you with its sublime implications, and another tear rolls down your cheek. You're overcome with a joy you have never felt before. You are overcome with acceptance and love for all that is, exactly as it is now.

Blissfully content, and feeling that your life could not possibly get any better than this . . . suddenly, again, you experience one more gigantic flash of illumination that nearly knocks you out of your chair . . .

As good as life now is, as joyful as you now feel, it has suddenly dawned on you that forever and ever and evermore, things will only get better . . .

Whoo-hoo, you have arrived! The promise has been delivered, your birthright accepted, and thy personalized kingdom come!

You Can Do It: Pop Quiz!

I trust you've paid attention, read every word up to this point, and that you're more than ready for this question:

Is life fair?

And the answer, which you've probably already blurted out, is: *Heck, NO!*

*Life is most certainly not fair! The cards are so heavily **stacked in your favor**, you have but to think a new thought and mountains move, help is sent, and worlds are born. It's almost as if you're cheating!* You are *so* poised for greatness!

A NOTE FROM THE UNIVERSE

Do you remember learning to ride your first bike? How impossible it seemed at first? Yet how impossible it now seems to ever imagine it was once hard. Well, thriving within the illusions of time and space is like that too.

First, you checked it out from the sidelines, then you dreamed of your own, and the next thing we knew, off came the training wheels. And I dutifully, dotingly, and reluctantly let you go, while galloping breathless at your side, as you let rip one wicked, "Hands-off!"

And so I watch. Beaming with pride over your first solo trips. Impressed beyond belief with your courage and determination. Stunned by your natural talent and ambition to grow. Humbled by your willingness to risk a fall. Comforted by knowing that you are exactly where you most wanted to be. And stretching even my own vast mind as I ponder and contemplate just how far you will go.

Ride on, brave heart, ride on.
The Universe

PS—You will be home for dinner won't you?
All of your favorite things will be waiting.

Fellow adventurer, it's been my great honor and privilege *to share the truths that I've shared with you* in *Manifesting Change.* I love you. I care. And I'm looking forward to the time when our paths will cross again in the jungles of time and space.

With every best wish, *tallyho!*